To James and Tom, who have always asked lots of questions

EFFECTIVE
INTERVIEWING

EFFECTIVE
INTERVIEWING

2nd edition

a handbook of skills and techniques

robert edenborough

KOGAN
PAGE

First published in 1996
First paperback edition published in 1999
Second edition 2002
Reprinted 2004

Kogan Page Ltd
120 Pentonville Road
London N1 9JN
United Kingdom
www.kogan-page.co.uk

Kogan Page US
22883 Quicksilver Drive
Sterling VA 20166-2012
USA

British Library Cataloguing in Publication Data

A CIP record for this book is available from the British Library

ISBN 0 7494 3755 3

Typeset by Saxon Graphics Ltd, Derby
Printed and bound in Great Britain by Clays Ltd, St Ives plc

Contents

About the author

Dr Robert Edenborough is a principal consultant in the Executive Search and Selection Division of KPMG in the UK. He heads the Management Review and Assessment Practice there. He previously led the Consulting Practice at ASE – a leading test publisher and prior to that was principal consultant with MSL, the international recruitment and consultancy specialists. A chartered occupational psychologist, Robert Edenborough has considerable experience of designing and applying interviews in organisations as diverse as the Ministry of Defence, the NHS and a range of financial service institutions. He has held senior posts with several major international companies: Head of Psychometric Testing and Assessment in ICL (1978–84), Managing Director of Selection Research Ltd (1984–89) and Head of the HR consulting division of Oasis Management Consultancy (1989–91). A regular contributor of papers at various international conferences, Dr Edenborough is also the author of *Using Psychometrics* (Kogan Page).

List of figures

Preface

I started specifically to think about a book on interviewing while preparing my previous book; *Using Psychometrics* (Kogan Page). I had been struck then by the fact that although there were obvious opportunities for linking different systems for studying other people, these were rarely grasped. The various gaps, overlaps, redundancies and complementarities among, say, a three test psychometric battery and a standardised interview process, tended not to be articulated and seemed little understood. This got me thinking about interviewing as such more widely. Why are conventional selection interviews so much maligned and so widely relied upon? Was it because all of us, not just psychologists, are experts on people? Do journalists' interviews, the questioning of witnesses and the use of a tasting panel to try out a new ketchup recipe have anything in common? Are all of these interactions simply more or less specialised forms of that important part of everyday communication: asking and answering questions?

In fact my concentration on interviewing pre-dated the thoughtfulness arising from writing about psychometric tests. I had been working for some time with criterion-based interviews for managers. Originally this work had been focused on assessment centres where this form of interview was being used as much as anything to help cover competencies not seen as readily assessed by exercises. (Staff development was one of these.) I then became exposed to the very different techniques involved in conducting counselling interviews. This included an intense period when I had central responsibility for performance improvement and redundancy counselling for managers. This was followed by my first exposure to what I have labelled the Structured Psychometric Interview (SPI) in which questions and interpretative guidelines are carefully researched and rigidly applied.

All of these cases had in common the idea of focusing upon the individual, helping to make decisions about him or helping him to make decisions about himself. However the generality of the interview situation struck me as I considered the range of circumstances in which I had used interviews to gather information from individuals, but to inform decisions that did not affect them directly. Thus as an applied experimental psychologist I had conducted debriefing interviews as part of laboratory experiments and equipment trials. Latterly as a management consultant I had also used interviews to establish competencies, plan climate surveys and to tease out scenarios for use in development centres. I became aware, too, that for many of those whose jobs I was studying – from salesreps to lawyers – interviewing was an important part of their working or professional life.

The aim of this book, then, is to provide a view of interviewing practices and phenomena to aid the manager or personnel specialist as practitioner. In nearly all work settings better understanding of others, whether candidates, peers, subordinates or clients, makes for better results. By casting the net of practice quite wide I have endeavoured to provide reference points for those whose practical concerns do, in fact, include interviewing, but who may not have had the opportunity to give much thought to interviewing methods as such. By indicating some of the links, continuities and pervasive issues in interviewing I hope I shall also provide some stimulus to the serious or amateur student of psychology or other fields of social science.

To seek to cover all interview usage in a single volume would be unrealistic if not impossible. What I have essayed in this book is to cover a broad sweep, focusing in most detail on those types of interview where I feel some of the insights of personal experience may be of use to the reader, but hopefully underlining throughout the very generality of the interview situation.

Preface to the second edition

As I endeavoured to demonstrate in the first edition of this book, the field of interviewing is undoubtedly ancient in its origins. Indeed, it is inextricably bound up with a whole range of human discourse and so virtually coeval with language itself. Against this backdrop, then, one might regard it as presumptuous to assume that half a decade or so should have given rise to major changes in theory or practice in this field. Yet some changes there undoubtedly are. For example, although it is arguable as to how far and in what way the Internet has had an impact on interviewing *per se*, it and other aspects of remote communication will undoubtedly continue to make **some** impact on interviewing as in so many other fields. (Indeed it could be argued that it is these very developments in communication that are now at last bringing about some aspects of the dystopian fiction of the first half of the last century from Zamyatin's *We* to Orwell's *Nineteen Eighty-Four*.)

Inevitably, there are also changes in associated fields such as psychometrics and assessment centres that will have an impact on interviewing practice and views. So too will different attitudes to aspects of work and the role of selection for a job as opposed to giving guidance on aspects of careers in general, which is increasingly becoming part of the interviewer's focus. Other developments include interest in studying whole groups of individuals in situations such as mergers and acquisitions, assessing the capability of the whole team and grasping the implications in 'human capital' terms of what can be revealed. The interview is the foremost instrument here because of its familiarity and lack of intrusiveness, with the scope to go where other techniques may fear to tread.

Again, even if there were no need for this type of updating there is certainly a need for continuing to sound messages of what interviewing and perhaps, in particular, structured interviewing is all about. As manifest of this no less a sophisticated organ than the *Financial Times* trumpeted ideas about structured interviewing in the current year (2001) as if it had made new discoveries, whereas in fact the approaches being described were being practised in some assessment and selection circles from the 1940s if not the 1930s onwards. Thus there seems to be a continuing need to declare what interviewing is and has been about!

Acknowledgements

I should like to thank MSL for support and encouragement in preparing this book. Although I had been working with interviews for many years prior to joining them I have found a more varied range of interview applications gathered under one roof than ever before. Working with colleagues in activities as diverse as executive search, client satisfaction studies, counselling, telephone screening and the design of role-play exercises has provided inestimable experience and scope for much practically focused debate. I should, however, point out that the views expressed are my own, and are not to be taken as necessarily representing those of the MSL Group or any of its subsidiaries.

Among colleagues who deserve particular mention, Jessica Beresford and Ian Foster saw through the production of the diagrams. Doug Prior provided detailed suggestions on the early chapters of the book. Antoinette Baker made valuable comments on the chapters on conventional and structured interviewing. Gareth Bennett-Coles and Sue Jackson both provided helpful insights for the chapter on counselling. Peter Sandham and Valerie Wilson both supplied ideas. Andrew Harley supplied references and made a number of useful suggestions on sources. The second edition of this book has been drafted since I joined the Executive Search and Selection Practice at KPMG. I should point out that the views expressed are, again, my own and should not be taken as representing those of KPMG. I am grateful for encouragement and support there from Colin Grant-Wilson, Katherine Huggard and Sharon Bick.

Among others who volunteered information or responded readily to my requests, I should like to mention Professor Alan Clarke, formerly of Hull University, Professor Clive Fletcher and Helena Thomas of Goldsmiths' College, Dr Jonathan Hill of the Gallup Organisation, Angela Mulvie of Wellpark Consultancy, Dr David Dance of the Royal Marsden, Nicholas Taylor of Epsom College and writer Paul Mungo. Barry Cushway engaged in discussion on many of the ideas represented. Barbara Phillips has worked cheerfully, efficiently and promptly to type an erratic and frequently changing script. My sons James and Tom and my niece Penny made a number of suggestions on content. Last in order, but first in support is my wife Marion. She has not only tolerated my hours of study and withdrawal from domestic concerns, but has helped throughout by reviewing and commenting on the text and, most importantly, by giving this enterprise her wholehearted endorsement.

to hold, as 'twere, the mirror up to nature

Hamlet

1

The place of interviews

THE INTERVIEWING SCENE

A range of settings

A recruitment consultant and candidate sit on comfortable sofas in an office. The consultant refers to a series of notes he has made from the candidate's CV and says, 'I see that you have had experience with X, Y, Z technology, but I'm not clear what your responsibility was for the project that your company was running. Can you tell me a little more?'

A line manager enters a syndicate room in a management training centre, briefly greets an interviewee and enters into a series of questions from a prepared list, covering the competencies of staff development, strategic planning and orientation to change. Occasionally she asks follow-up questions and probes. She makes notes continuously throughout the discussion.

A personnel officer picks up the telephone and explains to the person at the other end that he is working with a prepared interview and would like to tape-record his responses. After agreement the interview proceeds. Occasionally the interviewee asks for clarification, to be told gently, 'however you would like to respond is okay'.

An outplacement counsellor sits and listens while the man before him enters into a diatribe about the organisation that has just decided to make him redundant. After a while the counsellor says, 'Your feelings are quite natural and understandable. What we should be working with among other things is helping you to set them in context and so use that energy that you are showing now in relation to your future job search.' He does not intend to take the discussion very much further on that occasion.

A financial consultant explains to a couple in their living room that if she is to advise them professionally she must explore a number of aspects of their background situation and establish their needs. They nod in agreement but at the end of the session she will ask them to sign a form indicating that they have actually understood her role and agree to her advising them.

A group of four people assemble behind a green-baize covered table. Two of them, including the chair of the meeting, are elected council representatives with the others being the director involved and the personnel manager. In an adjacent room a candidate waits knowing that she is the first of three people to be seen that morning. She is invited in, motioned to a chair and the questions begin.

A patient enters a GP's surgery. He looks up; 'Good morning Mrs X, how are you today?' He has already noted the reddening mark under the patient's left eye and wonders if this will even be mentioned by her and if so if it will be dismissed as, 'I bumped into a lamppost', and how far he will get in explaining that the 'something' she needs for her nerves is to be as far away as possible from her violent husband.

These, then, form some of the range of interviews experienced variously and commonly in the course of working and everyday existence. Questions, answers and listening are common. They vary in the degree of pre-planning and structure. They are also differentiated one from another in the general form that they will take, the expectations of the parties involved and the skill level of both sides. They are all recognisable as types of interview and as such are themselves only distinguishable by a series of slow degrees from other forms of interaction involving speech. The 'Can I help you?', 'What size do you take?' and 'Can you wait a week for the alteration?' are questions familiar to anyone shopping for a garment. 'Why are your grades so poor?', 'Would you do better with another French teacher?', are examples relating to a parent interviewing a child on her school report. These shade into the even less structured 'Where have you been?' from the parent, which may signal the start of a lecture, or the 'Can I help you?' from the employee, slightly suspicious of the stranger wandering the office corridor.

We ask questions, that is we *interview*, to find out about other people, their attitudes, behaviours and skills or to tap into the information they possess. We believe that what people say tells us a lot, an idea neatly encapsulated by Wrenn writing in 1949. He said, 'Language is the expression of human personality in words . . .'

The interview as such is perhaps just a specialised form of what humans spend large proportions of their time doing, ie talking to one another by means of questions and answers. Although specialised, interviews are common. They are themselves a sufficiently significant part of human interaction that interviewing skills may be regarded as a set of fundamental life skills, practised with varying degrees of effectiveness but found at every turn.

PLAN OF THE BOOK

In this chapter I review some of the origins of interviewing and comment on different types of interview, indicating any links and differences. Comparing and contrasting interview methods and ideas will be a recurring theme throughout the book. It has struck me forcibly that, despite the common origins of different types of interview, links and contrasts are rarely drawn and are little understood. This view is reinforced by my finding, when preparing for this book, that books supposedly quite broad in matter such as Smart's *Selection Interviewing* (1983) or Taylor and O'Driscoll's *Structured Employment Interviewing* (1995), seem rather to push a particular and surprisingly narrow range of techniques. In this chapter, too, I briefly consider aspects of interviews other than what is said, including so-called body language, as well as some other ways of finding out about people.

Because selection interviewing is undoubtedly so mainstream an application and a considerable point of focus for the likely reader of this book, I have devoted three chapters to that subject. I have tried to explain and, again, link the various techniques and question some of the routine assumptions. In Chapter 5 I deal with those interviews related to performance management and enhancement. Counselling interviews, which are the subject of the following chapter may, of course, take place in work or other settings. I concentrate on the former but touch on some of the other uses as well.

In Chapter 7 we move to those interviews that are not necessarily focused upon the individual being interviewed but, rather, on using his or her responses to build up a body of information. This includes the specialised topic of survey interviewing. Chapter 8 is a review of a range of interview applications from the journalistic to the exit interview.

Chapter 9 is reserved for views about the future of interviewing, again seeking to set it in the context of overall communications among people. A number of sample interview passages are given throughout the text of the book, to illustrate the various types of interview discussed.

DEFINITIONS AND ORIGINS

Interviews defined

Roget's *Thesaurus* lists interviews in connection with hearing, listening, enquiry, exam, examination, interrogate, along with heckle, find out, quiz, pick one's brains and conference, all of which seem to imply some degree of formality in discourse.

The *Oxford English Dictionary* (*OED*) tells us that the word comes from the French *entrevoir*, to have a glimpse of. It goes on to expound the early common use of the term in relation to meetings, particularly of a ceremonial nature, such as the meeting between Henry VIII and the French King Francis I at the Field of the Cloth of Gold in 1520.

The journalistic use of the term is also quite widely covered in the *OED*. Thus it gives the *Palmall Gazette* of 1884 as quite dispassionately stating, 'Interviewing is an instance of the division of labour. The interviewee supplies the matter, the interviewer the form.'

The very common modern usage of the term, in relation to selection and associated applications which exists today alongside the journalistic interview, is of relatively late origin. It is absent from many dictionaries prior to the 1960s, even though modern interview practice pre-dates that period by many decades. A generally accepted definition, in relation to modern use, would be as follows; 'a meeting of people face to face, as for evaluating a job applicant.' This specific form is given in *Collins Dictionary* of 1981.

Ancient roots

The rather relentless questioning of one party by another or others, what we would now call interrogation, is undoubtedly ancient. Among other examples the *viva voce* examination was, for centuries, the standard way of examining undergraduates in the universities. As well as still being used for this purpose quite generally for higher level degrees (as discussed in Chapter 8), this methodology has clearly much in common with modern selection interviews, particularly of the formal board or panel interview type.

Formal questioning was, of course, an integral part of the procedures used by the Inquisition set up by Pope Innocent III under the
Congregation of the Holy Office in the thirteenth century. Such
processes although, of course, often abused, could result in uncover-
ing substantial tracts of information. This is nowhere more vividly
indicated than in Ladurie's (1978) account of life in a French village,
Montaillou. This detailed compilation is based upon inquisitorial
examinations conducted by Jacques Fournier, Bishop of Pamiers at
that town and Carcassone in the late thirteenth and early fourteenth
centuries. As we have seen, though, the idea of the interview for
selection purposes is more modern. Literary accounts of hirings in
earlier times are sometimes amusing, as in Dicken's portrayal of
Pickwick's acquisition of Samuel Weller, but rarely suggest a
comprehensive method for exploring the merits of the candidate.

'We want to know in the first place,' said Mr Pickwick,
'whether you have any reason to be discontented with your
present situation.'

'Afore I answer that 'ere question, gen'lm'n,' replied Mr Weller,
'I should like to know, in the first place, whether you're a-goin'
to purvide me with a better.'

A sunbeam of placid benevolence played on Mr Pickwick's
features as he said, 'I have half made up my mind to engage you
myself.'

'Have you though?' said Sam.
Mr Pickwick nodded in the affirmative.
'Wages?' inquired Sam.

'Twelve pounds a year,' replied Mr Pickwick.
'Clothes?'
'Two suits.'
'Work?'

'To attend upon me and travel about with me and these gentle-
men here.'

'Take the bill down', said Sam emphatically. 'I'm let to a single
gentleman, and the terms is agreed upon.'

The former lack of system in interviewing may, of course, be because patronage and recommendation were at one time a common basis for making hiring decisions. In *The Three Musketeers*, Dumas' account of Dartagnan's candidacy for the King's Musketeers hinges upon a letter of introduction from his father to their captain M. de Treville. The occasion of the theft of the letter *en route* to Paris is one of the pivots of the novel, and its absence when the hero presents himself to de Treville is a significant mark against him.

It was, in fact, only in the second half of the nineteenth century that merit rather than patronage was determined to be the criterion for recruitment by as significant an employer as the British Civil Service. The Northcote Trevelyan report of 1853–4 recommended that a Civil Service Commission be set up to oversee recruitment and promotion by competitive examination. This was made mandatory in 1870, but even then did not apply to the Foreign Office.

Modern instances

Modern interviewing can be seen as having several strands. The need for formalised techniques in selection was clearly recognised during the two world wars. The first of these gave a boost to paper and pencil psychometric instruments but little to interviewing practice as such. World War II saw the origin of the War Office Selection Boards (WOSBs) with their emphasis on an overall system in selection and with associated research flagging problems with unstructured interviews (see Vernon and Parry, 1949). Highly structured methods began to appear in the 1950s with the work of Clifton and his associates in the United States. They arose after experimentation with other techniques in which perceptions of other people were used to give clues to behaviour patterns (see Clifton *et al*, 1952). Specialist selection firms such as Management Selection Limited (MSL) emerged in the same decade, with their professional staff spending much of their time conducting selection interviews.

A significant but not generally acknowledged strand in modern interviewing can be attributed to Sigmund Freud. He considered that much of what people said could be related to unconscious drives and motives, exploring those as day-to-day occurrences in *The Psychopathology of Everyday Life* (1901). In terms of modern counselling and related techniques the work of Carl Rogers is critical. He advocated the importance of objectivity and acceptance in the counselling interview process. His *On Becoming a Person* (1961) is widely regarded as a central work in this connection.

Recommendations on selection interview techniques started appearing in print in the 1950s (eg Rodger, 1951), and there are today a variety of books on the subject (eg Fletcher, 1986; Anderson and Shackleton, 1993). There is also a substantial research literature, with a survey as far back as the 1940s (Wagner, 1949) being sufficiently extensive to have been dubbed by Anderson (1992) 'a major review'. In other uses of interviewing, too, advisory and research literature has been in existence for decades: for example, Oldfield's (1953) booklet *Fruitful Interviews* gives advice to Welfare Officers on dealing with their clients.

The use of interviews in staff surveys can be traced back to the 1930s, with Raphael's (1944) paper reflecting ten years of such work. The 1930s also saw the advent of political polling interviews, with the work of George Gallup in the USA. Other interviewing developments are more recent; for instance Morgan, writing in 1993, claimed that the focus group technique, which we discuss in Chapter 7, was virtually unknown to social scientists five years previously. As the various methods and applications unfolded some developed along crossing or parallel lines, while others diverged.

INTERVIEWING PROCESSES

Commonalities and variations

Questions and answers are, of course, common to all interview processes but there are enormous variations thereafter. At one extreme we have the pre-determined set of questions, which may explore particular areas and could be seen as functioning rather like a checklist. This may apply to strings of questions used in selection or, indeed, in other forms of interviewing such as the financial consultants' fact-finding. (An outline of such an interview is given in Figure 1.1.) By contrast we have the more open interview formats as used in counselling. In these cases there may be a need for the interviewer to probe, using a seemingly stray remark as a trigger for further follow-up and discussion. The memory load on the interviewer in the counselling case is much more demanding than in the fact-finding case. An episode in a counselling interview is illustrated schematically in Figure 1.2 (page 9).

It has been found that using the interview in selection does not

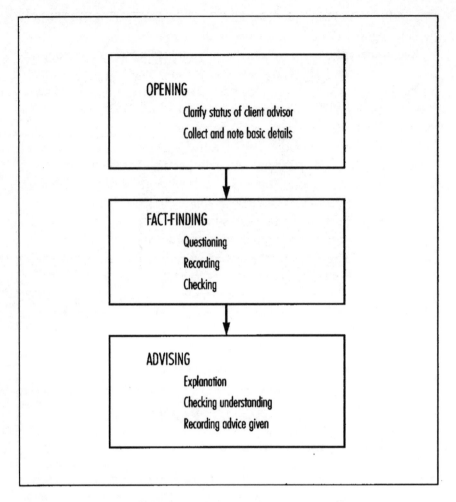

Figure 1.1 *Interviewing with a pre-determined structure, financial advice*

work very well and many writers on interviewing (eg Herriot, 1987; Bevan and Fryatt, 1988) have speculated on reasons for its continued use. Awareness of limitations in selection interviewing as commonly practised was one reason behind the development of structured techniques, which are discussed in Chapter 3.

Who takes part

Another variation in interviewing is in the number of people involved on one occasion in the interview process. Whereas by far the most

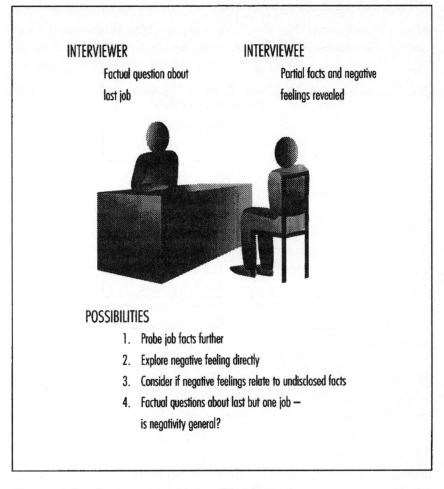

INTERVIEWER

Factual question about
last job

INTERVIEWEE

Partial facts and negative
feelings revealed

POSSIBILITIES

1. Probe job facts further
2. Explore negative feeling directly
3. Consider if negative feelings relate to undisclosed facts
4. Factual questions about last but one job –
    is negativity general?

Figure 1.2 *Options in a counselling interview*

common situation for any purpose is the one-to-one interview, panel
interviews are also widely used with numbers of interviewers ranging
from three to perhaps eight. Another common approach is the two-to-
one interview. Here it is quite usual for one interviewer to ask the
questions and the other to take notes – roles which may be inter-
changed in the course of the interview.

Another substantial variation is when there are one or two interviewers and a whole group of interviewees. This is typical in the
focus group interview, which may be used for market research
purposes or in situations in which it is required to explore a job and
develop a picture of competencies for it.

There are, of course, different practices in different cultures and societies. For instance in New Zealand, as exemplified by the recruitment and appointment practices of the Univeristy of Waikato, applicants are entitled to *whanau* support at panel interviews. *Whanau* members are friends or relatives of the candidate entitled to speak about the candidate at the interview and to ask the candidate's questions of panel members.

CONSCIOUS VERSUS UNCONSCIOUS

The attractive world of body language

It is often claimed that a large amount of information conveyed in communications relates to matters other than specific verbal content. This includes so-called paraverbal behaviour, such as tone of voice and hesitations in speech, and also non-verbal behaviour such as posture. Experimental studies relating to posture go back as far as the 1930s with the work of James (1932). The implications of posture have also been examined in connection with clinical states for many years (eg Deutsch, 1947).

This whole field of body language is clearly intriguing to many. Research by others such as Argyle (1975) shows that someone's physical gestures, mode of sitting and other aspects may tell us much about them. However, there is often confusion at the level of practical use as to what is fact and what is fiction in this, and very often interviewers will make fairly gross references to body language and draw their own conclusions without this having any particular basis in research fact. Claims are often made as to the proportion of information delivered by the various aspects of communication. Walmsley (1994), for instance, quotes figures to the effect that 55 per cent of communication is due to gestures and expression, 38 per cent to voice and only 7 per cent to words used. This appears to be derived from Mehrabian's (1972) book on non-verbal communication, but the content of the study is unclear and indeed Mehrabian's work is not formally referenced by Walmsley. I have come across frequent, albeit even less specific, reference to this same finding among the folklore of British management trainers and find it intriguing how such things can apparently become a received wisdom.

In a review of research on non-verbal behaviour in interviews Arvey and Campion (1982) concluded that such behaviour did influence the evaluations made by interviewers, but to a lesser extent than did candidates' verbal behaviour. Along the way they came across quite wide variations in findings. However, much of the research involved either quite drastic manipulation of non-verbal behaviour in experiments. One such (McGovern and Tinsley, 1978) manipulated energy level, eye contact, voice modulation and fluency together and not surprisingly found a difference in response to candidates exhibiting high versus low levels on all of these variables. This study and many others in this field used videotapes of interviews; some used static photographs of people wearing different expressions (indeed the original work by James (1932) used photographs). It cannot be assumed of course that this would translate into real-life responses of interviewers in the same way. Little, if any, of the research in this field has looked at strictly objective validation of inferences drawn. For instance Gifford *et al* (1985) in one study on the use of non-verbal cues by interviewers compared their ratings with self-rating by interviewees. Nor does the research clearly discriminate between non-verbal indications of short-term states – such as an anxious frame of mind during the interview – and long-term behavioural patterns – a general inclination to be anxious. Altogether it may be that interviewers tend to judge some characteristics such as social skill quite consistently from non-verbal behaviour, but this is different from these consistent or reliable judgements effectively predicting interviewees' future behaviour.

Looking the part

There is also the question of appearance and presentation, which is likely to include conscious and unconscious elements. At one extreme the interpretation of and weight put upon these aspects can become uncomfortably bound up with issues of equality of opportunity and prejudice against people, for example of a particular skin colour, age group, social class or region. At the other end of the scale, though, the clues to a person's transient state or mood indicated by their physical appearance may be seen as relevant to their short-term success in a job. There is also the notion that someone who has not bothered to dress up for a selection interview may be careless about or uninterested in the job. However, the converse does not apply necessarily: the candidate who appears neatly brushed and pressed, perhaps after careful grooming and checking by a partner, may not manage to present the same demeanor routinely. The danger of reading too much into such information is reflected in a distinction drawn by Wernimont and Campbell (1968) between signs and samples of behaviour. The former are unitary pieces of evidence, say the grubby shoes or the hesitation over a relatively common technical term. Samples are representative sets of behaviour which can be seen as forming a clear pattern directly linked to requirements of a job.

A range of conscious and unconscious indications is illustrated further in Figure 1.3.

OTHER EXCHANGES

Before moving on to consider our main interview areas in detail in the following chapters, I will briefly note some other ways of finding out about people, some of which do and some of which do not use questioning methods.

In selection situations a variety of techniques are used. Quite often there is a parallel between a conventional interview and what is contained in a CV or application form. In both cases people may indicate their work experience, formal qualifications, their skills, what interests them about the post, and their expectations and personal circumstances. Sometimes the exchanges in an initial interview are seen as merely exploring points that are not clear from the CV. Thus interview and documentation can be regarded together. Counselling may also make use of documentary material, such as biographical questionnaires, in conjunction with interviewing processes.

Psychometric tests typically used in work settings will explore abilities and personality variables. Reports on these may relate them to behaviours relevant to the job and as such they may also parallel what would be attempted in an interview. In my book *Using Psychometrics* (Edenborough 1994) I indicated some of the areas where there may be such parallels. An interesting case is the use of the interview to follow up on indications from a psychometric measure. This may apply in counselling or in selection where a clue to a line of enquiry may be given by a psychometric test. Such follow-up might be conducted by an interviewer skilled in the particular psychometric instrument, or by someone guided by the psychometric specialist with regard to what questions to ask.

There are other exchanges which are, of course, undoubtedly interviews, but where the scope is very narrow. The standard security

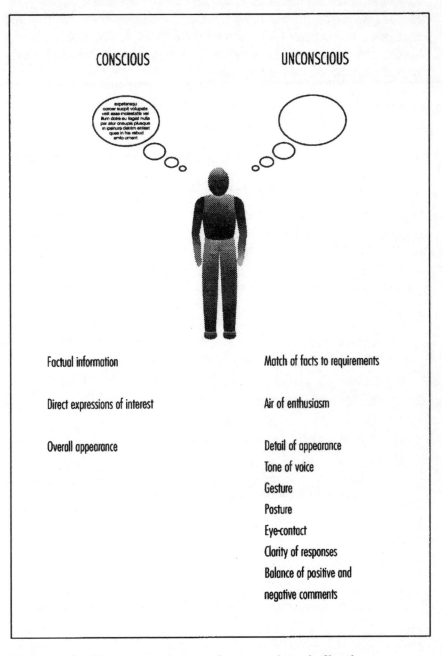

Figure 1.3 *Some conscious and unconscious indications in interviews*

questioning during check-in at an airport is an example of this type. (So too is the enquiry made of members of the audience entering the theatre to see the *Rocky Horror Picture Show* – 'Do you have any rice?', 'Do you have a water pistol?' – it being customary for patrons to bombard the players in this piece.)

SUMMARY

1. Interviews are widely applied and form a significant part of many interactions among people. They are sufficiently important for interviewing to be regarded as a life skill.

2. Originally applied to meetings and then to journalists' enquiries, the term 'interview' in connection with selection and other applications is relatively modern.

3. The use of interviewing in selection, though now common, was not so in the past where patronage and personal recommendation were routine.

4. Systematic selection interviewing techniques with varying degrees of structure began to be developed in the 1950s with links back to methods used in World War II.

5. Counselling interview techniques can be traced back to Freud, with modern counselling owing much to Carl Rogers.

6. Limitations in the effectiveness of selection interviewing are well established, but interviews remain popular.

7. Although, regardless of application, the one-to-one face-to-face interview is the most common form, multiple interviewers and/or multiple interviewees will be found in some circumstances.

8. Verbal content is the main focus of attention in most interview situations, but non-verbal information, especially body language, is sometimes examined.

9. In selection and in counselling other sources of information, including psychometric tests, are often used together with interviews.

2

'Conventional' selection interviewing

INTERVIEWING IS POPULAR

A strong assumption

As indicated in Chapter 1, despite the fact that selection interviews are perhaps criticised more often than almost any other area of management functioning, they remain popular. They are so popular that nearly everybody writing about interviewing refers to this fact in parallel with the reiteration of the problems and limitations associated with them. For example Anderson and Shackleton (1993) describe the selection interview as 'favoured and expected'. Eder and Ferris (1989) refer to the emphasis in practice on the unstructured interview as 'one of the ironies of employment practice'. In reviewing research on a wide range of methods used in selection, Robertson and Smith (1988) grouped conventional interviews in a low, but positive, band of validity. They appeared in company there with references, personality questionnaires and interest inventories. They were ahead of handwriting analysis, for which no validity was demonstrated, but below assessment centres and grouped ability tests.

Many such writers go on to indicate techniques that can improve what I refer to here as 'conventional' interviewing. In this chapter I will also make a substantial commentary of this nature, indicating what can be done to enhance the effectiveness and accuracy of judging the qualities of candidates for jobs through this means. However before doing so it may be worth considering both the popularity of the interview process and what I call a 'strong assumption'.

The strong assumption is simply that in interviewing for selection some form of conventional interview will almost always take place and be a central part of the selection process. By conventional interview is meant one in which a person's past career and present interests are explored in a fairly unstructured way. This type of interview is usually conducted one-to-one and nearly always face-to-face. The interviewee will often be given the opportunity of asking questions of the interviewer who may, in any case, volunteer information about the opportunity and the employing organisation.

This assumption is given a further tightening twist by researchers on interviewing who often refer to the interviews they study without declaring them to be structured or unstructured. There is then a tacit, or perhaps very properly called 'default' assumption, that unless most clearly stated otherwise 'interview' equals 'unstructured interview' (see, for example, Ramsay *et al*, 1997).

It is not uncommon for organisations to be very pernickety on the one hand about the costs they may be incurring in, say, an associated activity such as recruitment advertising, but to be totally unaware of and unconcerned about the processes used and the amount of management time involved in conventional interviewing. Thus organisations may tolerate the time and effort involved in conventional interviewing without really seeking any particular review of cost-effectiveness or the adoption of good practice to improve matters.

There is, of course, the question of what might be gained by other approaches. Despite my involvement in psychometric procedures and my advocacy (Edenborough, 1994) of the range of information these can uncover, I am aware that psychometrics alone will not necessarily give the totality of information required for accurate selection. Thus a battery giving readouts on a wide range of personality dimensions and exploring intellectual functioning, even if supported by a documentary listing of qualifications, would not tell one what the *specific* motivations were at the present time for a candidate. Nor would they indicate – and perhaps this is one of the major points in favour of conventional interviews – how previous experience might bear on the present job. Thus the strong assumption seems likely to continue to be made.

Nevertheless, the need for conventional interviews has sometimes been challenged, often with enduring results. For instance, in the 1960s Clarke set up an experiment in which half of the students for a psychology degree course were selected on the basis of the Universities' Central Council on Admissions (UCCA) application form, and no interview, while for the other half interviews were used. Tracking results in terms of academic grade performance over a five year period showed no differences between the two groups. He concluded (Clarke, 1996) that the interview conducted added nothing, except in the case of mature students where additional information might be important. Today, with far more students applying for university, places are frequently offered without interviews having been conducted.

Most interviewers are lousy, but I will interview

There is a widely accepted view that interviewing, like driving or making love is something that most of us think we do better than most other people. Although there is no direct research to support this view, as opposed to the evident widespread commitment to interviewing, it is well sustained in myth and popular self-deception. Certainly, in my wide experience of discussing interview techniques, including developing a range of interview protocols and associated processes I can count few who would admit that they were a lousy interviewer. I have, though, found many people who have felt that their interview technique could be improved by training. Perhaps this is half a step along the path to better things.

There is another point, though, which may be more telling than the apparently universal claim of superior skills in interviewing. There seems to be a need for reassurance about the interviewee, which can be gained by interaction with them, and which cannot be fulfilled by any other means! Part of this apparent requirement for direct knowledge of the other person is undoubtedly related to liking. If you have to work with someone over a period of time and you dislike them on first acquaintance then this may be hard to reverse and feelings of dislike might better be dealt with at the interview stage rather than when the contract of employment has been signed. Quite often, liking will be related to aspects of sociability which some studies (eg Otis *et al* 1962) have indicated as being capable of correct prediction from interviews. Whether or not these same sociability factors predict success on the job is another issue and many other studies (see again Bevan and Fryatt, 1988) suggest that for many jobs it does not.

Very often, of course, one is picking out a range of unconscious indicators which may not even be capable of being articulated as such. Today, in comparison with several years ago, few might admit that even though they may not actually require candidates to have been to Oxbridge, they ought to be able to present themselves as though they had. The conventional interview represents the best way to explore such impressions. These ideas may be seen as related to the notion of implicit personality theory: people undoubtedly have different subjective models and views of personality, so many are inclined to use only their own model in understanding another person – and how better to test them against that than by meeting them in the interview?

The pervasive nature of prejudice in interviewing and the fact that it may be applied unconsciously by the interviewer were both partly demonstrated in a study by Awosunle and Doyle (2001). In a laboratory setting they played tapes of interviews to white and black raters. The content of questions and answers was the same in each case but those rated as candidates had either Afro-Caribbean or East London accents. The black raters rated the black candidates higher than the white and vice versa. The authors saw this as showing potential for 'institutionalised racism' in interviewing, noting the findings as particularly disappointing with most of the rater subjects being students 'at a university which tries very hard to celebrate diversity'. The unconscious influence of what would, objectively, be evident as irrelevant factors was found in a study by DeGroot and Motowidlo (1999). They found a positive relationship between a number of aspects of interviewees' voice quality, such as pitch and rate of speech with interviewers' ratings.

There is also, of course, the question of specific hypothesis-testing. Sometimes in chains of interviews one person will feel that they have inadequately explored a particular aspect or there is some lingering doubt that requires further investigation. The second interviewer then is charged with exploring this. This may apply, too, in an interview following receipt of a CV; does a gap in the sequence of employment reflect long sick leave, unemployment or a typographical error?

Two perspectives

One of the sources of apparent lousiness in selection interviewing may arise from two quite markedly different perspectives on the whole interview process. In one there is a push for a rational and systematic gathering of data about the candidate, with a step-by-step building up of the picture. This approach is particularly strongly reflected in the whole of structured interview methodology, which is the subject of the next chapter. However, a systematic approach also colours many effective conventional interview practices discussed below.

An alternative view is that the interview is just as much about selling the employing organisation as it is about finding out about the candidate. Central to this view is the idea of the overall fit between employer and employee. Associated with this is the notion of the value of each party having the opportunity to gain an intuitive feel for the other, and that rigidity in interview processes severely limits this opportunity.

Many psychologists writing on interview research seem to recognize the superiority afforded by structure in interviewing. As Boyle (1997) points out though, unstructured interviews conducted by untrained people who don't know what they are looking for are still 'too common'. Yet there are some who defend the unstructured position. Thus Oliveira (2000) discusses the view that there is a logic to unstructured interviewing with some managers able to apply implicit knowledge based on wide experience of their own organization when they opt for unstructured interviewing. (It may perhaps be questioned as to whether their 'opting' is in itself conscious or, more likely, the pursuit of an implicit and possibly institutionalized approach.)

These differing models have been labelled by Anderson (1992) as the objectivist-psychometric and the subjectivist social-perception perspectives. He sees the distinction as important in shaping the research that has been done on interviews. It is also important, too, in shaping the practical approach taken to conducting interviews, even if not clearly acknowledged as such. Thus those with a strong objectivist-psychometric approach would see the subjectivist-social perception approach as woolly. Those who propound or practise the latter tend to see the objectivist-psychometric approach as overly remote, or, as one recruiter put it to me on a structured interview course, 'Something dreamed up by HR people and nothing to do with the real business of recruitment'. Given that these two different positions are not often clearly articulated – in these or equivalent terms – it is perhaps not surprising that the perception is more often just that others do it *wrong*. (As Dr Johnson said, 'orthodoxy is my doxy; heterodoxy is another man's doxy'.) However, it is also possible for the two approaches to operate together, particularly when multiple interviews are used.

Many of the observations below can be seen as reflecting the objectivist-psychometric perspective primarily, the subjectivist-social perception approach being necessarily less capable of prescription. The bad practices as represented particularly by the horror stories at the end of this chapter are to be avoided from whatever perspective or model one might be operating.

HOW TO DO CONVENTIONAL INTERVIEWING

Setting and settling

Arvey and Campion, in their 1982 review of employment interviewing, indicate a variety of factors separate from the interview structure as such which need to be considered in an interview programme. These include the role of the interview in the selection system and the proportion of interviewees likely to be hired. They also include the physical setting. A controlled environment in which to conduct an interview is needed, and this is something which nearly all writers on interviewing recognise and acknowledge. There is, though, sometimes debate on how much time should be spent in social niceties or chit-chat before the interview starts. If this is totally ignored then the start of the process may seem overly abrupt: if it is protracted before the interview proper starts the interviewee may wonder if a range of enquiries about her weekend activities is actually a subtle part of the interview and may be unnecessarily on her guard. There is some value in checking out immediately preceding activities. People who have had a difficult journey may be overly focused upon this if they do not have the chance to clear the issue. Those who have been passed on from another party may not necessarily have had their expectations set as to what is to happen on this particular occasion or what is to follow. Again, some scene-setting as part of the introductory process can be valuable. Certainly freedom from interruption should be assured, both as a courtesy and in terms of maintaining an appropriate degree of concentration by both parties, if the interview is to be taken seriously.

Question types and formats

There are a lot of recommendations in writings on interviewing about question types with many firm and sometimes contradictory statements being made. Setting aside the structured interview cases (which we will be exploring in greater detail in the next chapter) the following are some of the points that arise.

Leading questions

A leading question is one in which the response is assumed. 'Don't you agree that . . .' would be the typical introduction to this type of question, which may go on to state something like, '. . .you should be able to do everything your staff can'. The possibilities open to the interviewee faced with such a question are several. He may simply acquiesce, in which case little is gained, or he may contradict the interviewer. He may see it as something of a challenge and regard a contradiction as what is required regardless of his own feelings. It may be that the topic is something that he has not considered before and putting the question in this rather blunt way may force him to express some view while in reality he holds none in particular. A more neutral question would be, 'Some people say that a manager should be able to do everything that their staff can, while others say that this is not necessary and may incline the manager to get trapped in detail. How do you feel about that?'

Closed questions

Similar difficulties arise with other forms of closed question, ie those that only admit of specific answers such as 'yes' or 'no'. However, although many writers and teachers of interviewing practice inveigh against these, they can be particularly useful in clearing particular points out of the way. As such they may relate to matters of fact not already established, perhaps through prior documentation. Examples of useful closed questions are, 'When did you work on product X?', 'How many people reported to you?', 'Did you have direct or functional responsibility for the accountants in division Y?', 'How long did it take to develop that plan?'

Open questions

Open questions are often recommended by writers on interviewing (eg Lewis 1992) as a means of generating information. These invite views: 'What are your opinions on...?', 'How did you find X...?', 'What was it like at...?'

These are likely to make up the effective bulk of most conventional interviewing. However, they do suffer from the danger that they may lead to an overly discursive response by the interviewee. Variations may be made on the most open format so as to narrow the scope somewhat, as in: 'Tell me about the challenges you have faced at work recently', and 'What sort of people did you interact with when you were selling product y?'

Probing and challenging questions

There is also the probing question, which may be used for getting further information. It may in itself be open or closed. Examples of the former are 'Tell me about that' or 'How' or 'Why' questions. An example of a more closed probe would be, 'Were you selling to the personnel function or to the line?' It is sometimes said that too many probes can make people feel that they are being interrogated, and so feel uncomfortable. This is also the view of the questions or responses actually designed to put people on the spot. These include 'I disagree with that', or 'Why do you hold that view?' One text on interviewing (Leeds, 1988) recommends asking candidates if a particular statement that they have just made could itself be directly checked out with referees. There is little reason for going down this track and such an approach should be reserved for cases where there may be a real question of doubt as to the truthfulness of the respondent.

Reflecting

Another form is the reflecting question, in which the interviewer plays back to the interviewee what he has said. In fact it is often likely to be in the form of a statement rather than strictly a question as such. Sometimes this is done to cover matters of fact, as in the following:

Interviewee: Then I was given a larger group to manage, which meant I just could not stay as close to the coal-face day-to-day. Management by wandering about alone was just not enough, so that I really found myself obliged to clarify reporting lines and put in regular review procedures.

Interviewer: So having to handle a larger group of people meant you had to structure your approach to management much more?

Alternatively reflection may turn more upon matters of feeling, as in the following:

Interviewee: At that time I had just moved further away from the office, which I might not have done if I had known about the changes in working hours. I found I often had to cope with travel delays quite late in the evening. It seemed that no one in the company had thought of that. My immediate boss, who didn't have the same sort of family responsibilities as I had, didn't want to know and Personnel just quoted the rule book. I might have been more inclined to stay if someone had shown interest or at least recognised the problem, instead of that I seemed just to be fighting the company all the time and that didn't seem like a good basis for a long-term working relationship.

Interviewer: So you felt that the company was unsympathetic to you?

In both cases the interviewer's response shows that they are listening, thereby building and reinforcing rapport. In the first passage the interviewer's response is likely to lead to a further exposition by the candidate as to what he did, and in particular to result in quite clear statements about his own particular role in the process of structuring. A closed question such as 'Did you actually decide that yourself or were you told to?' could lead to defensiveness and/or a stock answer, 'It was my decision', rather than the fuller exposition prompted by the reflection. A simple open question, such as 'Tell me more', might well lead to a discursive exposition. It is not clear whether the more required is about the problem arising from the increased staff or the solution to it, or both. 'Tell me more about what you did' is more directive without being as likely to cue the interviewee as the closed 'Did you actually . . . or . . .' above.

In the case of the interviewee with problems of working patterns and travel, the reflection, although neutral and entirely non-evaluative, could serve to legitimise the feelings of not being sympathised with. This is likely to lead to further expressions of feeling, which may give a useful slant on the candidate's tendency to become stressed or upset. A closed question at this stage, such as 'Did you leave because of that?', is likely to shut down this line of enquiry. An open question in the form 'How did you feel about that?' may also be less powerful here. Although it does open the door to further expressions of feeling it may suggest to the interviewee that her feelings, which she might see as to some extent obvious, have not been adequately received. The reflection more clearly recognises the feelings that have been voiced.

The question of reflection in interviews is returned to again in Chapter 6 on counselling interviews. In conventional selection interviews a mix of open and closed questions and reflective statements is likely to be most useful.

The use of CVs and application forms

Very often an interviewer will have access to a CV or application form in advance of conducting an interview. Carefully used these may be valuable props. Expressions of interest in a particular job or career phase may establish rapport and also establish an area for exploration of certain skill areas. Thus if a candidate has held one post in which she had responsibility for large numbers of staff and another in which she was part of a small corporate think-tank, exploration of the former is likely to yield the more fruitful information about the candidate's abilities in people management. Getting her to contrast her views on the two roles may indicate the type of work that satisfies her more and so could provide a fairly sustained source of motivation.

The initial examination of CV or application form information may provide a variety of other clues for areas to explore. These could include claims of special achievements on the one hand or, on the other, gaps or inconsistencies that need to be clarified. However, to make a rigid review of CV and application form content as such in the interview may simply be to reproduce unnecessarily the information contained therein.

Information-giving

There is quite a lot of debate about using the interview as a setting for giving information to the interviewee. Indeed another reason for the evident popularity of the conventional interview is that it does give the interviewee the occasion to ask questions. If there is a constant to and fro of questioning though, any line that the interviewer is pursuing is prone to lapse. Attention may be broken and the interviewee may, himself, gain information for use in response to questions in later parts of the interview. Also although information-giving can be seen as a standard aspect of the subjectivist social-perception view of the interview, discussed earlier, there is a clear potential for a form of mutual halo effect, in which each party comes to a satisfying but inaccurate view of the other. This is illustrated diagramatically in Figure 2.1.

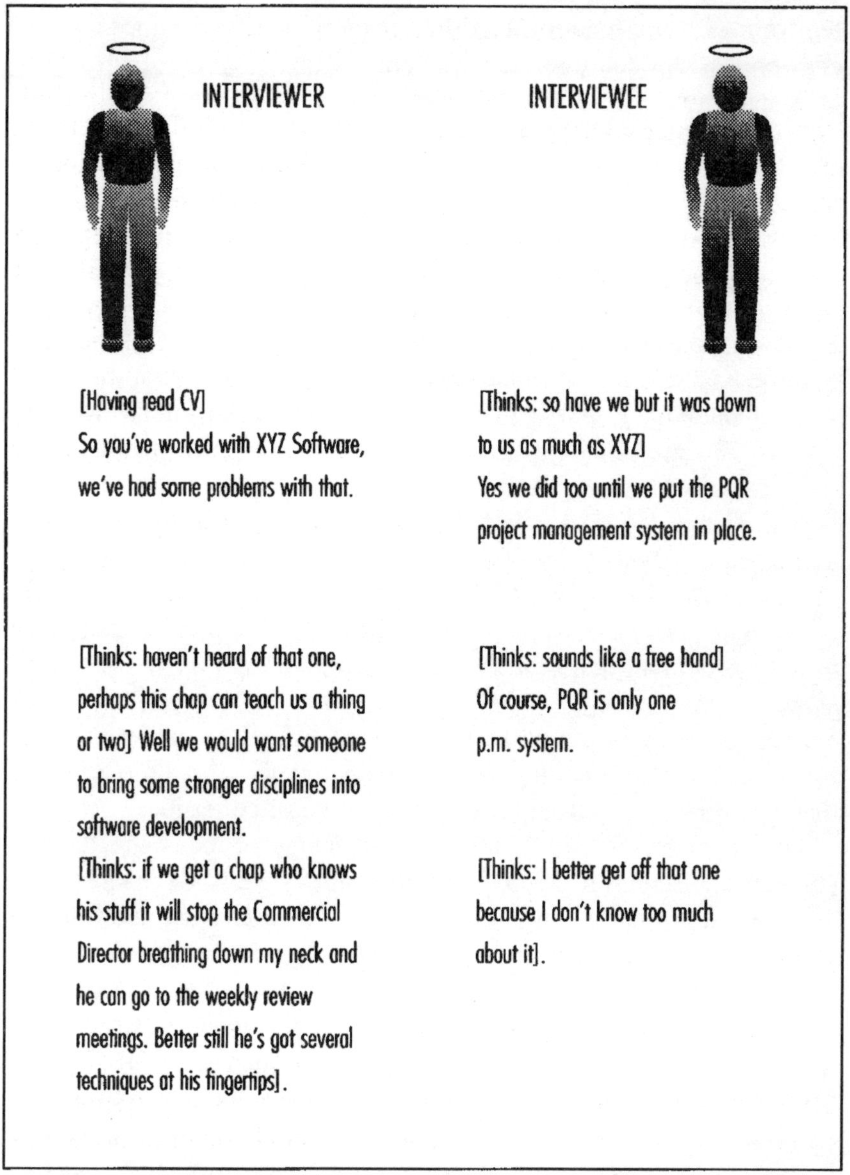

INTERVIEWER

INTERVIEWEE

[Having read CV]
So you've worked with XYZ Software,
we've had some problems with that.

[Thinks: so have we but it was down
to us as much as XYZ]
Yes we did too until we put the PQR
project management system in place.

[Thinks: haven't heard of that one,
perhaps this chap can teach us a thing
or two] Well we would want someone
to bring some stronger disciplines into
software development.
[Thinks: if we get a chap who knows
his stuff it will stop the Commercial
Director breathing down my neck and
he can go to the weekly review
meetings. Better still he's got several
techniques at his fingertips].

[Thinks: sounds like a free hand]
Of course, PQR is only one
p.m. system.

[Thinks: I better get off that one
because I don't know too much
about it].

Figure 2.1   *The mutual halo effect*

One approach to avoiding some of these difficulties is to reserve set times in the interview for giving information. If there are intended to be a series of interviews in a half day or day this may be done in the form of a presentation or in the form of setting up question and answer sessions for interviewees. This is one way in which objectivist-psychometric and subjectivist social-perception approaches may to some degree be combined.

INTENTION AND PRACTICE

Common difficulties

Many mistakes can occur in interviews and perhaps one of the most common is just not to take enough trouble over the setting and stage management arrangements. It is common for interviewees to appear unaware of the position of a particular interview in a whole recruitment process, who they are to see, or any special preparation that they are meant to have undertaken. If a CV has not been requested in advance, letting people know if you do or do not want to see one at the interview is courteous. It may avoid candidates fumbling in briefcases and trying to take you line for line through a written document that you do not particularly want to peruse at that stage.

Freedom from interruption seems more difficult to achieve than to intend, and actually unplugging the telephone may be more effective than any form of electronic gating or briefing of colleagues.

The interview process is about an exchange of ideas and there is sometimes discomfort on the part of the interviewer if there is a pause. The typical way of filling such a pause is to restate the question. Of course if the question is restated it is likely to add little to clarity and may even confuse. Another common approach is the portmanteau question, which puts forward a series of propositions. A portmanteau question followed by a pause – because it is confusing – followed by a restatement of the portmanteau issue(s) may leave the interviewee feeling that she is now being required directly to demonstrate intellectual powers rather than review, perhaps, some aspect of her career or experience!

An effort to cover all aspects of an issue in the question may confuse:

Interviewer: Can you tell me how much responsibility you had in that project? That is, were you in charge of planning and execution or just, you know, part of the project?

Candidate: (pause) Um, er, well.

Interviewer: Sometimes there can be a split responsibility, or maybe different responsibilities at different times for different things, say in a complex project with several phases, so did you have the whole thing all the way through or was it the different parts at different times?

In the example in the box above it was probably not necessary for the interviewer to add anything after saying the word 'project' for the first time.

Another area of some debate and contention is that of note-taking during interviews. Some interviewers – I suspect sometimes the lazy ones – excuse themselves from ever taking a note on the grounds that it would be distracting to the interviewee and make it difficult for them to maintain eye contact and otherwise show that they were listening[1]. Certainly the head down approach and constant scribbling all the way through may be disconcerting and the skill of making appropriate notes in a conventional interview is something that will have to be practised. Note-taking does appear to aid accuracy. Schuh (1978) manipulated note-taking – permitting it or not – and interruptions, and found the highest accuracy when note-taking was permitted and there were no interruptions.

Perhaps the largest area of difficulty is actually that of listening. It is exacerbated in those situations where there is no pre-planning or in which there is a constant feeding of information back to the interviewee rather than assimilating what has been said by the interviewee.

---

[1] It might be argued that the distinction between the two perspectives discussed above would be reflected in the degree of rigour applied to note-taking. This is not necessarily the case. Reference to an effective record may subsequently help clarify or remind the interviewer of the feelings experienced at the time. Letting the interviewees see that their views and questions are being noted may instil more confidence about the seriousness with which their candidature is being taken than if it appears that memory is to be the entire record of a one-and-a-half hour discussion.

Another problem area lies in the physical setting of the interview room. What is interesting here is that different sources actually disagree as to the appropriateness of different room layouts for conventional interviewing. While most seem to agree that facing directly across the table is uncomfortable and challenging, there is considerable disagreement as to whether it is or is not appropriate to interview across the corner of the table, sitting in comfy chairs or at round tables. Some of the views on arrangements are illustrated in Figure 2.2.

On top of these difficulties and problems there are, of course, a range of horror stories. While some of these are undoubtedly the matter of myth rather than reality – such as the comic incident portrayed in Richard Gordon's *Doctor in the House* in which the unfortunate candidate mistakes the gender of a woman attired in a rather masculine style and loses his chances of appointment by calling her Sir – there are many real ones. The stories in the following section are from my own experience or those of immediate colleagues, all but one as relayed at the time of their happening. The generality of such experiences is reflected, too, in Anderson and Shackleton's (1993) speculation that all their readers would be able to recount personal experience of poor treatment by a selection interviewer.

INTERVIEWING HORROR STORIES

1. A candidate was interviewed by the personnel director for an internal post on a day on which major employee-relations trouble was anticipated and indeed broke. An hour's interview was interrupted no fewer than 13 times by phone calls or people coming in with messages. The interviewer did apologise for the disruption but did not offer to reschedule the meeting to an occasion when he could do a proper job of it!

2. Two managers were interviewing a candidate who used a piece of jargon, 'At that time I was using the gobbledygook software system for project management' he said. 'What is that?' asked one interviewer. 'Surely you know that' asked the second interviewer of his colleague. The first interviewer glowered 'Yes I do, but I want to see if she does' he said!

3. It was the university milk round. A bored interviewer saw that his next candidate was studying music and French and he was cross

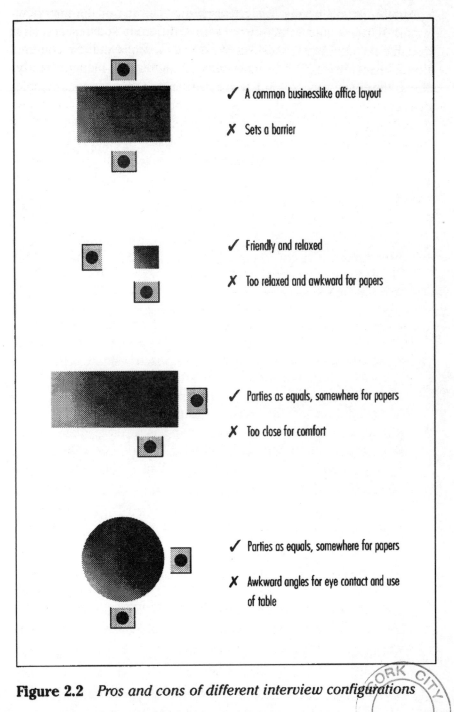

Figure 2.2 *Pros and cons of different interview configurations*

with the sifting process for having produced someone so obviously unsuited for work in a technically-oriented company. 'I see you study music and French' he said. The candidate nodded enthusiastically. 'Then sing the Marseillaise' the interviewer requested.

4. Interviewers not being present themselves for the appointment arranged on their behalf is almost commonplace in some organisations. The next story unfortunately is a not atypical exchange which actually took place with a candidate and one of the world's leading firms of executive search consultants. A candidate presents himself (as requested by the sign at the office entrance) to the security officer on the front desk. 'I am John Bloggs to see Sue Smith'. The security officer looks through lists. 'Have you got an appointment? I'll phone through, what did you say your name was, look she ain't here, they're sending someone out, do you want to leave a card or something? Are you sure you've got an appointment? What did you say your name was?'

5. The two-person interviewing team had discussed the forthcoming day's interviews rather too enthusiastically the night before. One, rather the worse for wear, gulped some black coffee and then launched stoically into some questions. The other interviewer picked up a pen and made notes, wincing at the sound of shuffling paper. After a quarter of an hour the note-taker nudged the questioner and whispered in their ear, 'You've just repeated your first three questions'.

6. In an interview on Wall Street one of two interviewers stood up and leaned over the desk towards the candidate and said, 'If I picked you up by your collar and threw you against that wall over there what would you do?' He replied, 'Nothing'. When asked, 'Why not?', he said 'Because you're bigger than me'. The candidate was later told that he didn't get the job because he didn't have the killer instinct.

7. A woman interviewed for a job in an ice-cream factory was asked when her next menstrual period was due. (This story does date back to 1961: it couldn't happen today – or could it?)

SUMMARY

1. Conventional unstructured interviewing with a career history focus is very widely practised, despite quite general recognition of its limitations.

2. The opportunity to make a direct personal assessment of a candidate and to gauge personal liking, whether explicitly or implicitly, appears to underpin the continued use of the conventional interview.

3. The objectivist-psychometric view of interviewing stresses the need for hard evidence gathered in a systematic fashion. The contrasted subjectivist-social perception approach stresses the need for gaining an overall intuitive feel for candidates as well as selling the employing organisation to them.

4. The overall handling of the interview should include clarity as to what is to be expected there and at any subsequent stages of selection. The environment should be controlled and the interview conducted without interruptions.

5. Leading questions should generally be avoided and challenging questions used sparingly. Open questions are effective in opening up an area for discussion or in exploring a candidate's views without giving out clues to looked-for answers. Closed questions may aid clarification of specific facts, but may limit scope for establishing a candidate's views. Reflecting responses back to a candidate can help clarify facts or encourage the revelation of feelings.

6. The use of CVs or application forms may help direct interview questioning fruitfully.

7. Giving information freely in the interview may underpin rapport, but may disrupt information-gathering as well as cueing the interviewee as to desired responses.

8. Common difficulties in interviewing are experienced with:

    - the stage management or control of the process
    - handling pauses
    - framing questions clearly
    - note-taking
    - listening
    - physical layout of the interview room.

3

Structured interviewing in selection

SCOPE OF STRUCTURED INTERVIEWS

Structured interviews run all the way from simply more organised approaches to conducting the conventional biographically based interviews, as described in the last chapter, to instruments which, in their form, lie very close to what would normally be regarded as psychometric measures. A major study of interviewing in selection (Wiesner and Cronshaw, 1988) found much higher levels of validity for structured versus unstructured methods. It is possible that the large differences they found still understated the situation with regard to interview practice. To be in a position even to be included in a study implies some degree of system, whereas many employment interviews are still practised along the lines of the horror stories included at the end of the last chapter. (Thus McDaniel *et al* (1994) in a meta-analytic study reported 'even the unstructured interview was found to have a respectable level of validity'. However their conclusions appear to have been based on public sector interviews with fairly clear criteria and often the use of rating forms ie a degree of structure. Indeed, they state that 'the typical interview in the private sector is likely to be substantially less structured...'.)

Perhaps the earliest, but still widely-used form of structured interview, is the approach advocated by Rodger and encapsulated in his Seven-Point Plan (NIIP, 1951) (see box). This was a way of planning an approach to an interview to ensure that a number of aspects of a person, seen as generally of relevance, were explored. A comparable scheme was the so-called five-fold grading system of Munro-Fraser (1954).

THE RODGER SEVEN-POINT PLAN

1. *Physical make-up* Have the candidates any defects of health or physique that may be of occupational importance? How agreeable is their appearance, bearing and speech?

2. *Attainments* What type of education have they had? How well have they done educationally? What occupational training and experience have they had already? How well have they done occupationally?

3. *General intelligence* How much general intelligence can they display? How much general intelligence do they ordinarily display?

4. *Special aptitudes* Have they any marked mechanical aptitude? Manual dexterity? Facility in the use of words or figures? Talent for drawing or music?

5. *Interests* To what extent are their interests intellectual? Practical? Constructional? Physically active? Social? Artistic?

6. *Disposition* How acceptable do they make themselves to other people? Do they influence others?

7. *Circumstances* What are their domestic circumstances? What do other members of their family do for a living? Are there any special openings available for them?

THE FIVE-FOLD GRADING SYSTEM

1. *Impact on others* Physical make-up, appearance, speech and manner.

2. *Acquired qualifications* Education, vocational training, work experience.

3. *Innate abilities* Natural quickness of comprehension and aptitude for learning.

4. *Motivation* The kinds of goals set by the individual, his or her consistency and determination in following them up and success in achieving them.

5. *Adjustment* Emotional stability, ability to stand up to stress and ability to get on with people.

Increasingly, with the legal requirement to avoid discrimination, and the emphasis on achieving 'political correctness', commenting on physical make-up as advocated by these schemes could be regarded as suspect. Armstrong (1995) refers to the use of schemes such as these as typically following the specification of requirements. Even so, their prescriptive nature in regard to areas likely to be irrelevant could operate against any careful requirement specification, in addition to being seen as intrusive or potentially discriminating. Today many employers will, in fact, proscribe questioning in areas relating to background where the specific relevance of these has not been confirmed. (Arvey (1979) reviewing legal cases involving discrimination in the USA found that one consistent theme was the questioning of women about marital status, childcare and related issues, areas of inquiry not put to their male counterparts.)

The focus on behaviour

With other forms of structured interview there is less emphasis on building up a general picture of a person and more on exploring specific behaviour. Thus in the interviews to be discussed under criterion-based and critical incident methods below it is evidence of relevant behaviour that is sought directly. Interestingly, though, in what can be regarded as the most advanced form of structure in interviewing and which is being called here the structured psychometric interview or SPI, the emphasis again may be in some cases away from specific behaviour and more towards tendencies to behave. These latter are established in a variety of ways including specific instances, and also by asking a range of questions aimed at tapping into attitudes of which a person may be only slightly or scarcely at all conscious. Thus structured interviews would most generally be seen as lining up with the objective-psychometric model of interviewing, using Anderson's (1992) distinction between that and the subjective and social-perception approach discussed in the last chapter. However, the SPI may sometimes in effect break this distinction down by spanning the two sides of the divide.

The fact that structured interview techniques cover such a broad church is a complicating factor for those seeking to evaluate methods or decide on appropriate means to use in selection. Thus we have on the one hand methods where the specific content of the interview has been arrived at by careful and painstaking research and where those using the interview are required to go through rigorous training which can last up to a year. On the other hand we have the output of what might be a Friday afternoon huddle to discuss areas for questioning and not backed at all by any form of training or check on standards. Although it is contended here that structured interview methods may give considerable benefits and increments in accuracy that can make them, perhaps, the most cost-effective of all methods likely to be used in selection, their design and use requires considerable care. Certainly, as in fact with conventional selection interviews, the warning 'rubbish in, rubbish out' applies with some force here, so we turn next to a range of approaches to producing structured interviews. As the particular case of the structured psychometric interview (SPI) is gone into in considerable depth in the last part of this chapter only passing reference will be made to it in the following section.

Of the methods and concepts referred to here, several have applications elsewhere, too. Thus we shall refer again to the repertory grid in Chapters 6 and 8 and to focus groups in Chapter 7, where job specification is also again referred to.

DERIVING INTERVIEW MODELS

The repertory grid

One of the most powerful techniques established for determining relevant dimensions to explore in interviews is the repertory grid. This is by no means used exclusively for definitions to be fed into interviewing practice and it is a methodology that can be used in connection with assessment centres or counselling situations. It has been employed in a wide variety of settings with applications including those in the field of market research and even in areas such as the derivation of dimensions to describe the handling characteristics of military aircraft.

The repertory grid was developed by Kelly (1955) in connection with his *Personal Construct Theory*. Much has been written about it since, a lot of it highly technical in nature, but Bannister and Mair's (1968) book is still a good general text on the subject. The repertory grid (or rep. grid as it is often abbreviated) is a way of sorting out the concepts or constructs a person uses to describe a particular area of interest. In the case of selection the area of interest would be the characteristic behaviours or attitudes relating to a particular job.

The method involves getting those who are knowledgeable about the particular area – the job, in this particular case – to go through a sorting process in which they can articulate the relevant dimensions. A variety of tasks may be used for this purpose but a simple and the most commonly used one is a card-sorting method. First of all the interviewee is asked to list a number of people currently performing the job or a similar one. Numbers from 8 to 12 are frequently used. The individuals are identified by the respondent to his satisfaction with a number being written down on a separate card to represent each individual. The interviewer then selects sets of three cards, usually initially at random. The interviewee is asked to group the cards in ways which indicate how two of the individuals represented are alike and different in some way from the third. The responses are noted. A second set of three cards is drawn and the process repeated. Further drawings are carried out either until all possible combinations are exhausted or until no new discriminating dimensions emerge. Thus very often part way through the interviewer is rapidly assessing which fresh combinations are likely to yield interesting distinctions.

Once the drawings of cards is complete the interviewer goes on to request the interviewee to rank-order the individuals who are being discussed. This rank-ordering is in terms of their effectiveness in the job of relevance. The result of this is then explored further to resolve any ties given. Specific behaviours are then explored further, building upon the distinctions originally rendered and looking at why particular behaviour patterns are important. Repetition of this process with two or three people who are knowledgeable about the role concerned can fairly rapidly home in on the dimensions of relevance. An example of part of a repertory grid interview output is given below.

A repertory grid interview

Interviewer: We are discussing the job of a level X manager in finance. Could you please identify for yourself eight level X managers whom you know. You should have a spread of capabilities among them. Write down their names or initials on a piece of paper for your own reference, and then just number them from one to eight. Okay?

Interviewee: Okay.

Interviewer: Now I have a set of cards also numbered one to eight to correspond to the people on your list. I am going to draw three cards at a time and show them to you. I want you to tell me a way in which two of them are alike but different from the third.

Interviewee: Okay.

Interviewer: Here are the first three, numbers two, three and five. Can you tell me a way in which two of them are alike, but different from the third?

Interviewee: Well, two and three are well organised with good attention to detail. Number five is, I guess, more entrepreneurial in style, and doesn't pay much attention to detail.

Interviewer: And the next three are numbers four, six and eight?

Interviewee: Four and six are strong people people, if you know what I mean, people managers I suppose, while number eight is much more focused on tasks.

Interviewer: And what about numbers one, seven and five?

Interviewee: One and five are quite strategic. Seven takes a much more short-term operational view.

From the questioning indicated here it appears that being organised, managing people and thinking strategically are three of the dimensions that the interviewee uses in thinking about financial managers in the company. Further exploration will yield further dimensions and reveal which the interviewee sees as most important. Comparison with other interviewees will show the degree of agreement among them.

Critical incident techniques

In this method the emphasis is upon those incidents that have been significant or critical in determining the success or otherwise in the job. By exploring these important turning points one may build a picture of those behaviours that are required for effective performance in the role, and where lack of the capacity to cope with a particular type of incident would be especially disabling. These situations then form the basis for structuring the interview itself as discussed later in this chapter.

The method was developed by Flanagan (1954) following earlier work (Flanagan, 1947), with World War II American bomber crews. Then, in what today would probably be called business process re-engineering, attempts were made to study the various activities and processes that were critical to a bombing mission. In his 1954 paper Flanagan defined an incident as 'any observable human activity that is sufficiently complete in itself to permit inferences and predictions to be made about the person performing that act'. He also set out systematic protocols for exploring incidents. Those questioned clearly needed to have detailed acquaintance with the incidents and were labelled subject matter experts (SMEs).

Job specification and job descriptions

A variety of methods are available for deriving job specifications and writing job descriptions. Some of these relate to scoping or sizing the job for remuneration purposes (see Chapter 7) but these themselves will, of course, be of relevance in determining the types of behaviour that may be required. Thus someone with financial responsibility over a very large budget will require to have those skills which reflect the prudent handling of money. Someone required to undertake long-range resource planning is likely to need to be able to conceptualise strategically and comprehend the potential interaction of a variety of issues some time into the future.

Sometimes job descriptions are derived directly from an initial specification of organisational structure and a definition of areas of responsibility alone and do not give direct indications of behavioural requirements. Sometimes in a job description there is a rather long list of responsibilities and accountabilities. These may need to be considered carefully in terms of the required behaviours that they imply. There may need to be a process of grouping of areas of activity very specific to an organisation before a clear enough picture of the behaviours can be gathered to construct an interview. Such a process is illustrated overleaf.

JOB DESCRIPTION FLEET MANAGER (EXTRACT)

1. Good contacts in the motor trade and, preferably, the finance houses.

2. Familiarity with practical aspects of maintenance workshop management.

3. Ability to interact with colleagues at all levels.

4. As a major budget holder, financial planning experience is essential.

1 and 3 may imply communication skills.

2 and 4 may imply control and review skills.

1, 2 and 3 may imply negotiation skills.

2 may imply staff motivation skills.

It may be difficult to produce an effective structured interview if the number of areas indicated in the job description is large. Similarly, whether or not a job description is produced, if a checklist of behavioural descriptions is presented to a recruiting manager it is not uncommon for nearly every area to be endorsed as relevant to the job. Clearly this complicates rather than helps the task of identifying *relevant* behaviours.

The essential simplifying process that techniques for studying and analysing jobs are meant to provide is neatly captured by Algera and Greuter (1988). They see this role as one of interconnecting between criteria of job performance and predictors of that performance, including interviews.

The role of competencies

The term *competency* sometimes seems to be simply a modern version of what may otherwise be referred to as dimensions, criteria, traits or even themes of behaviour. Its current usage can be attributed to Boyatzis (1982), who defined it as: a capacity that exists in a person that leads to behaviour that meets the job demands within the parameters of the organisational environment and that, in turn, brings about desired results. A similar definition from Evarts (1987) will be explored here. It runs as follows: A competency is an underlying characteristic of a person which is causally related to effective or superior performance in a job or role.

The various aspects of the definition are all of importance. Thus by referring to an underlying characteristic we mean something that is likely to be sustained, repeated and reliable over time. It is not however necessarily implied that this should be something absolutely fundamental to the person. Indeed, debates about the various contributions of nature and nurture do not need to be entered into when considering competencies. The term *underlying* and its implication of behaviour that is repeated is meant to remove one from the arena of superficial judgements. For example the person who appears with a button missing from her jacket at an interview may be habitually scruffy and pay insufficient attention to her personal presentation, or she may have been unfortunate enough to have caught her clothing on a nail while entering the interviewer's office. More information would be needed to determine whether she did in fact possess the competency of appropriate personal presentation. (This is, of course, akin to Wernimont and Campbell's (1968) distinction between signs and samples referred to in Chapter 1).

The *causal* part of the competency definition is to distinguish between those many characteristics which may be studied and measured about a person and those aspects which actually do provide a link to relevant behaviour. Thus having acquired a particular academic qualification may or may not be correlated with the capacity to perform a particular job. The qualification is scarcely likely – talisman-like – to cause the capacity for performance. However, a tendency to grasp complexity and to learn new facts and figures may well be part of the causal chain, and the competency would be expressed in these terms, not in terms of the possibly related qualification.

A focus on effective or superior performance is one which we shall return to again in some detail under Structured Psychometric Interviews. A moment's consideration may show that in building models of success one is far more concerned with what the successful actually do than with what the unsuccessful fail to do. In seeking to understand competencies required for piano playing one would learn little by watching and listening to an incompetent player striking the wrong notes! By contrast a period of study with an accomplished exponent of the instrument would be likely to expose the relevant characteristics of behaviour far more.

One may be forgiven for thinking that there is nothing very new in competencies and, rather like Molière's Monsieur Jourdain in *Le Bourgeois Gentilhomme*, who discovered he had been speaking prose for more than 40 years, the discovery of competencies as an idea is not particularly earth-shattering. On the other hand by referring any explicit or implicit model of behaviour to a definition, albeit as simple as that given, one may begin to sort the wheat from the chaff in deciding what range of behaviours and predispositions to behaviour are relevant. This can help avoid the trap of focusing on totally irrelevant or prejudicial aspects or seeking a very broad and over-comprehensive model as with the checklist approach mentioned earlier.

Competency descriptions may be expressed in a variety of ways. Sometimes they lead to very tight prescriptions which may apply very much to a particular job or class of jobs. Thus one comes across prescriptions such as 'must be able to draft policy documentation appropriate for consideration of directors of subsidiary companies'. In other cases they are more clearly rooted in behaviour. Two examples are given below. In the first a brief definition is followed by quite a detailed exposition and both positive and negative behavioural indicators are given. In the second, briefer, example only the positive behaviours are shown.

PERSONAL

Control of initiatives

Making decisions and taking charge of events
Executives strong in control of initiatives make a definite decision to proceed with an action or actions. They see themselves as owners of decisions and the actions required to stem from them. They may position a variety of others in representative or supportive roles, for instance using inputs from financial, ops or planning deputies, but they will be clear that it is they who are setting actions in train. They may see their work as a series of projects to be set in motion. They will take initiatives not only in

terms of making things happen, but also in the sense of self-management. They will be in control of their own time as a resource and will have distinct means of coping with the stresses of the job. They will be prepared to follow through tenaciously, not letting problems deter them and not succumbing to hostility. This competency is one that will be significant in the leadership style of the executive.

Positive indicators	*Negative indicators*
Can identify when a decision to proceed was taken	Vague about decision points
Takes charge of a range of activities – calling meetings, briefings, initiatives, planning	Lets activities 'take their course'
In charge of their own time	Event-driven
Statements indicating ownership personally or with or through immediate group	Ownership for actions resting with outsiders, maybe vague 'they'

Reproduced by kind permission of MSL HR Consulting Ltd

DIRECT INFLUENCING

Definition

The ability to convince others to buy something or to support a recommended course of action, and the ability to reach a compromise between two conflicting parties.

Behavioural indicators

- Persuades others by pointing out benefits to them.

- Uses information or data effectively to persuade others or support a position.

- Offers several different arguments to persuade or support a position.

- Explains complex ideas by using well-chosen examples from personal experience.

- Prepares for presentations with documentation, facts and figures.

- Anticipates and prepares for how people will react.

- Identifies the most important concerns and issues to others.

- Tailors own language to the level of audience.

- Makes a special effort to relate to people and their own level of understanding.

- Presents own position persuasively.

Reproduced by kind permission of MSL HR Consulting Ltd

In the UK the Management Charter Initiative (MCI) has had a considerable influence on the promulgation and currency of competencies (or competences in their preferred spelling). They make a distinction between these and underpinning knowledge and understanding. They see performance standards, defined as the activities and outcomes which constitute good performance, as depending on both knowledge and understanding and personal competencies.

CRITERION, COMPETENCY-BASED AND CRITICAL INCIDENT INTERVIEWS

There is a class of interviews where evidence is sought related to particular competencies or criteria. Criterion-based interviews actually have their origins in another field, that of assessment centre technology. It is from that field that the term criteria comes, a usage which pre-dates competency, though no practical distinction is made here between criterion-based and competency-based interviewing. However, a brief excursion into assessment centres is made in the next section. They are discussed in more detail in Chapter 4. The idea of exploring critical incidents as a way of establishing areas of relevance was discussed earlier in this chapter. The critical incident framework can also be used, in effect, as the script for an interview.

Assessment centre technology

Assessment centre methods grew out of requirement by various fighting forces during World War II to select young officers. In the British Army these became known as the War Offices Selection Boards (WOSBs) referred to briefly in Chapter 1. Comparable techniques were, though, used by the Office of Strategic Services in the United States, and by the German Army. Central to all was the notion that rather than using historic methods of selection, based very much on a conventional interview exploration of a person's background, it made far more sense to carry out some sort of simulation of the tasks with which they were involved. This led to the use of simple outdoor command situations in which young men would be given the task of leading a group of others in activities such as crossing a stream with ropes and pine poles carrying an oil drum with them. Such outdoor activities were boosted by internal tactical planning exercises that were paper-based. Commercial applications followed leading to a variety of methods such as the in-basket, in which a person's handling of correspondence is examined.

The need to interview

One principle of the assessment centre approach is that of using a multiplicity of measures in order to enhance reliability and to explore a variety of situations. Some of those situations were more extended in time than others, and the competencies associated with them – such as the development of staff – which might be very significant in a variety of roles, were relatively difficult to access by immediate exercise activities. Therefore the approach was used of asking interview questions specifically related to these competencies or criteria and then applying some degree of rigour in interpretation.

Typically the questions themselves are only partially pre-determined, giving scope for individual follow-up. The degree of licence that this might imply is not necessarily extreme. To begin with, part of the proper use of assessment centre methods involves the careful training of assessors. This training will typically include the practice of criterion-based interviewing and within this would be scope to explore and broadly agree interpretations. Also the assessment centre process involves a wash-up discussion in which information from a number of assessors is shared and their initial evaluations challenged among the group.

This again helps with standardisation; the assessor who has conducted a criterion-based interview on a candidate provides the evidence for his conclusions to his colleagues, and these conclusions are subject to revision in the light of the ensuing discussion.

An illustrative sequence of questions is shown below.

COMPETENCY-BASED QUESTIONS – DIRECT INFLUENCING

- Tell me about a time when you resolved a disagreement between two people.
  (If necessary)
  What was the source of the disagreement?
  Did the problem arise again?

- How do you get other people to do things?
  (If necessary)
  Can you give me an example?
  Was that something that they did not originally want to do?
  How do you know that?

- Think of something fairly technical or complex in your work; how would you explain it to a lay person?
  Can you explain it to me now?

As will be evident by reference to the panel on the direct influencing competency, many of the questions directly reflect the behavioural indicators given. Although derived from assessment centre technology, criterion-based interviews are frequently used outside the context of assessment centres as such, as stand alone methods.

The critical incident technique as an interviewing method

The idea behind the critical incident approach is that the response to some incidents may be critical in determining the success or otherwise of a job. The publican shouting time to a rowdy group of revellers and how the consequent strongly expressed desire to remain in the pub drinking was handled would be one example. Another might be pushing through a capital expenditure budget in the face of opposition in order to make a department viable.

The use of the critical incident technique to structure an interview is based on the idea of exploring the candidate's capacity to respond appropriately to the incident. There are variations on the style of the question used. In the so-called situational interview (Latham *et al* 1980) candidates are asked how they would behave in a given situation. Responses are rated using behavioural statements developed by experts in the job concerned (the subject matter experts or SMEs again) as benchmarks. Thus the immediate focus is on hypothetical behaviour. In the Patterned Behavioural Description Interview – PBDI or sometimes just BDI (Janz 1982) – candidates are asked about specific critical incidents again, but now in terms of actual experience. These two types are illustrated below.

CRITICAL INCIDENT INTERVIEWING

A situational question
You have been working on a product advertising campaign with a client for several weeks and have finally agreed the whole plan including all the copy. You have media space booked for three weeks ahead and have a photographer and studio lined up for product shots next week. Your client contact phones you and says that her boss's boss has just seen the copy and is not happy about some of the messages. What would you do?

A patterned behavioural description question
Have you ever managed to get to the nub of a resource allocation problem when others seemed to be floundering or casting about? Tell me about an occasion when you experienced this.

The distinction between these two types of critical incident interview is superficially that between the hypothetical and the actual. Taylor and O'Driscoll (1995) have emphasised this distinction in their book on structured interviewing, but the distinction is not absolute. In many cases one would expect respondents to the situational interview to draw upon what they had actually done. The two techniques can, in fact, be merged by the simple follow-up of 'have you ever experienced anything like that?' to a situational question. Rather similarly either of these types of question might be used in competency-based interviewing. Indeed the first example in the panel showing direct influencing questions could be regarded as a PBDI question.

Limitations

As with all interview methods there are some limitations in these approaches. Using the criterion-based interview technique in the context of assessment centre work requires a detailed understanding of that methodology. Using it outside an assessment centre may be to do so without the rigour implied by having a facilitator chairing a discussion and without the interplay of comment from a group of others.

With critical incident interviews an unskilled interviewer may give too many clues as to the area of exploration, may rephrase or paraphrase acceptable questions and in effect cue the interviewee to the right answer. Of course this happens, as indicated above, with conventional interviews but there is an added danger that perversely because of the very specificity of the criterion-based approach it may be more open to cueing than otherwise, because the situation is clearly defined.

STRUCTURED PSYCHOMETRIC INTERVIEWS (SPI)

Origins

The origins of the SPI approach go back to the 1950s in the United States. The SPI is predicated upon the notion that those who are the most effective exponents of a role – the most competent – actually talk about their work in ways that are different – perhaps qualitatively as well as quantitatively – from those who are not. There are some conceptual links, of course, between this idea and the illustrative behaviours that can be brought out in the criterion-based or critical incident interviews. Some links can also be seen with those areas relating to the idea of expression in speech being a fairly direct reflection of personality as referred to in Chapter 1 (Wrenn, 1949). It is this latter notion which, of course, is arguably at the basis of all interview methods but it is also arguably only with the SPI that its exploration is systematised.

The idea of speech as an indication of consistent patterns of behaviour is, of course, not by any means new. As indicated in Chapter 1 the whole matter of Freud's *The Psychopathology of Everyday Life* is full of links between what we say and our underlying attitude and behavioural tendency.

It is also noteworthy that methods aimed at modifying behaviour, even on an enduring basis and so arguably involving some modification of personality, concentrate on manipulating speech patterns. This is most graphically illustrated in George Orwell's novel *Nineteen Eighty-Four*. There two particularly powerful principles are applied in the controlled language 'Newspeak'. One is the explicit use of labels opposite in meaning from what they actually denote; the other is the contraction and so limitation in thought underlying the language. These concepts are both illustrated particularly in the abbreviations to 'Minipax' and 'Miniluve' of the War Ministry and Secret Police respectively. Arguably, also, the use of repetitions in religious ceremony, the chanting of slogans by political or sporting groups, can all be seen as tending to comparable ends. It is against this relatively complex background that the SPI should be seen.

Excellence modelling

As indicated, a key to developing an SPI is the modelling of excellence among the current exponents of a relevant role. This does, of course, assume that who is excellent can be known in advance but arguably in any form of modelling of effective performance the same requirement applies. It is likely to be somewhat easier, though not particularly easy, to discover in those fields where there are hard data. Thus in areas such as selling or other jobs involving measurable performance, for example control of materials wastage, there will be some objective measures. These measures may be complicated by a variety of other factors and usually it is as well to check the apparently hard data with more subjective information. For instance a salesperson working with a product group towards the end of its natural cycle will be disadvantaged in relation to colleagues already in a position to sell the latest types or models.

Once such excellent performing individuals have been identified it is usual to undergo detailed discussions with them, typically in focus-group mode. (The topic of focus groups is returned to in Chapter 7 in other connections.) The focus group is a semi-structured means of gathering views from a number of people all of whom can be expected to have something to contribute. Its use in relation to the SPI involves exploring attitudes, behaviours, situations and circumstances relating to the role, and how problems are overcome, what would be factors making for success and what would be likely to lead to difficulty.

The focus-group participants are asked to reflect on their own attitudes, behaviours and experiences and those of others, to characterise truly effective behaviour and contrast it with that exhibited by the mediocre or wholly ineffective. Usually such discussions are tape-recorded for detailed transcription. In analysing this material, in addition to the various pieces of information gathered on the circumstances, situations and behaviours of relevance, such as would apply to the critical incident and criterion-based techniques, one notes the particular use of words. Thus if a particular situation is spoken of with intensity or vividness, this may give a clue to attitudes supporting success which can then be reflected in the interview itself.

One-to-one meetings may supplement the focus group or groups but one does then lose the opportunity for the most effective practitioners themselves to thrash out differences in views expressed. Typical of an issue that might arise is consideration of whether the most successful salespeople in a particular field insist only on meeting the top person in an organisation, or is success related to having one's foot inside any door!

A number of questions are then derived from the information gathered. They are likely to be related to a tentative competency or dimension model. This question set and the model may be further fleshed out by additional one-to-one discussions, possibly with those in charge of the target group. More information may be added, too, from the study of relevant documentation such as mission statements, policies or business plans for extended periods of time ahead. From the questions generated on the basis of this material one would then trial a first version of the interview on another group of clearly expert exponents of the role, using their responses to further refine the questions and define the interpretative framework for them and the competency model. Sometimes this stage may be skipped as a specific step and collapsed with the following one, in which two contrasted groups are studied. One group will, again, consist of excellent exponents of the role. The other will be made up of those who are seen as less effective. By applying the interpretative framework to the responses of these two different groups one may see if the instrument is overall capable of discriminating between them and so be an effective tool in selection. As part of this process it is sometimes necessary and appropriate to discard quite a large number of question items. Once the interview has been developed in this way it is necessary to train those who are going to use it.

The amount of effort required in training will depend not only on the capabilities of those trained, particularly their degree of comfort in handling the complexities of language that may be involved, but also on the complexity and clarity of the coding frame used. There will be some cases where a fairly broad framework can apply to questions and others where the framework is narrower. For instance it is possible that a high-performing sales group will have distinguished themselves from their average colleagues by giving, say, three rather than just two examples of selling a new product in its first week on the market. This difference will need to have been captured in the interpretative frame-work and then reinforced in the training. ('Two examples may sound good so why not give the interviewee the benefit of the doubt?' Answer, 'Because if you do then you will tend to be selecting more like your mediocre, rather than more like your best.') Sometimes the questions show up relatively unusual responses which are characteristic of some of the expert group but not of all of them, so it is necessary to ensure that these are also captured in the interpretative framework.

Types of question and interpretation

The range of questions used in an SPI may be quite broad, corresponding to the PBDI and situational questions discussed earlier, as well as exploring attitudes and feelings or intentions: 'How would you feel if ...?', 'How would you endeavour to go about ...?' Some questions will explore simple matters of fact, while others will pose hypothetical situations. Some ask very open-ended questions – 'Tell me about ...' – while others are closed – 'Would you prefer X or Y?' The touchstone in deciding whether to include a question in the final format is always whether or not it produces different responses between the higher and lower performing groups that it is intended to distinguish.

In all cases an important tenet of the approach is that interpretation of the question is not given to the respondent. Although this may be thought of as an aspect generally applying to interviewing, for otherwise the interviewer might well be at least halfway to supplying the answer, it is particularly important in the SPI. Here the respondent is required to operate from their own frame of reference and it is recognised that this is likely to give the strongest clue to their typical or consistent behaviour. Adding to that frame of reference, for instance by illustrating an unfamiliar word, will tend to change the picture. For example the term 'equity' can refer to fairness and justice or to the shares of a limited company. The question, 'Tell me about the equity in your present company' might produce a response in terms of, say, equal opportunities consciousness or financial ownership. To elaborate the question by specifying which use is meant is to supply the frame of reference for the candiate – virtually to give the answer – rather than to tap into the interviewee's natural frame of reference, which forms the basis of each person's natural behaviour. Elaboration is tempting when the interviewee seeks clarification, but this at least distorts, if it does not wholly destroy, the value of the SPI approach.

Use and delivery of the SPI

As with a variety of other advanced techniques, such as personality questionnaires, there is little doubt that the SPI method is likely to fare best in the hands of specialists, either external consultants or a more or less dedicated group within an organisation. The former are often likely to be more comfortable in fulfilling a requirement to prepare narrative reports on candidates. Such reports can, in fact, be as detailed as those written on the basis of a standardised psychometric battery (see Appendix I). They may be particularly useful when the SPI is applied in development rather than selection, giving as they can scope to suggest development options that are likely to be effective.

Given the degree of standardisation inherent in the SPI it is not necessary for interviewer and interpreter to be one and the same. Just as two or three paper-and-pencil psychometric instruments might be administered by one person and interpreted by another, the same can apply to the SPI. This will often involve the use of a tape-recorder and the services of a transcriber, so that the person making the interpretation will work from a printed text of the interview. This also provides scope for further checks on standardisation in interpretation.

The standardisation of the process also means that a part of it can be clearly separated out and used as a shorter screening device, with the remainder of the questions being delivered only to those who pass this first stage. In this way time and money can be saved while still preserving the objectivity derived from the use of a common and highly specified process. Also questions in the SPI are frequently arranged so that competencies are addressed successively question by question. Thus if eight competencies are to be covered, the first of which is direct influence, questions 1, 9, 17, 25, 33 and 41 of a 48-question interview would seek to tap into this competency. This obviates the problem of cueing referred to above in connection with other forms of competency-based interviews.

The Structured Psychometric Interview is often delivered by telephone, an approach which appears to work well. It has the advantage of saving a large amount of time and money. It can sometimes appear unfamiliar as a method to candidates and appropriate briefing is necessary. This would often be done initially when an appointment for a telephone interview was booked, when expectations, for instance as to the time that might be required, would be set. The use of a standard introduction at the time of the interview is also important. This should cover, among other things, the important point discussed above that no interpretation of questions will be offered. It will also include gaining permission to make a tape-recording of the interview.

Reservations and caution about SPI

The training to work effectively with the method can be quite daunting and without it the technique rapidly defaults to a loose semi-structured interview. Training focuses on the delivery of questions as illustrated above, and also upon their interpretation. It is the latter which after initial difficulties with delivery are likely to pose the most problems. It is sometimes difficult to refer back to the original source of the interpretative framework and it is not uncommon to find manuals of SPI interpretation littered with year after year of amendments without any necessary basis in fact.

Caution by the uninitiated about the use of the SPI is typically based on the notion of what in Chapter 2 I have called a strong assumption as to what an interview should be. Telephone delivery has sometimes also been a cause of concern. The telephone is a piece of technology that has been with us for well over a hundred years and it is perhaps surprising that there should be any resistance to its use. In fact resistance is more often put forward by those with armchair experience of the method rather than those with direct familiarity with it. It does, though, indicate a further clear requirement for training if the interview is to be delivered in an efficient and confident way to the candidate.

Armchair critics are also much inclined to view any form of highly structured interview as overly mechanistic. For example Harris (1989) reviewed the so-called comprehensive structured interview (CSI) which comprised a mix of questions covering situational and job knowledge, job simulation and worker requirements. He concluded that this might be viewed as an 'oral version of a written test'. To retort, 'and why not add the rigour of testing to the comfortable medium of the spoken word?', might seem to line up too firmly on the objectivist-psychometric side of the debate between that philosophy and the subjectivist-psychometric one (see Chapter 2).

The SPI is such a broad technique that it is sometimes seen as universal in its application. No real limitations have yet been found as to the types of role that can be explored. My experience in the last five years alone has covered salesreps in a new insurance company, hybrids linking IT and business, middle and senior managers in the NHS, and North Sea oil-rig engineering supervisors. But of course the SPI does not directly assess current level of skill in a particular field any more than do other interviews or, say, personality questionnaires.

It is also sometimes assumed that it is just another interview and there is therefore a temptation to see it as only applicable at an early and crude stage of the selection process, whereas in fact it can yield data comparable to, say, a battery of psychometric methods. Again it has sometimes suffered by being put together with far less effective methods such as ill-thought-out presentations or poorly conducted conventional interviews.

Last but not least is the question of costs. Although when established the method is likely to be as cheap as other one-to-one methods and far less expensive than, say, full assessment centres, thorough bespoke research is required for it to realise its full potential. The training required if it is to be done properly is likely to be on a par with that needed for the interpretation of psychometrics. (But if training seems expensive, what price ignorance?) One may also need to consider the cost of having tapes typed up. All that having been said, both published studies such as that of Wiesner and Cronshaw (1988), Wright *et al* (1989) or Robertson and Smith (1988) and, from my own professional experience bespoke research, typically show structured interviews in general to have substantial validity.

Convergence on structure

There are perhaps a number of forces, some operating in specific fields and some more generally, that suggest structured approaches are here to stay. Although they may not wholly supplant conventional interviews across the board, they may, as suggested in Chapter 2 supplement the conventional approach or actually replace it in certain instances. First there is an increasing recognition of the very existence of structured interviews. As a consultant I have found clients increasingly aware of and familiar with such approaches. Thus discussions once characterised by questions such as 'structured interviews: what are they?' are now typified by 'structured interviews: what sort do you use?' Search and selection firms who would once have wholly anathematised a structured approach have more recently sought to include it as part of their unique selling proposition. The subsequent stage is its recognition as something routinely expected by clients and of commodity status.

Next is an increasing awareness, albeit varying in its specificity and intensity, of the ills attendant upon prejudice plus its pervasive nature as encapsulated in relation to one particular type in the term 'institutionalised racism'. This has prompted moves towards enhancing manifest objectivity in many aspects of employment. It has been a point of emphasis in recent literature on interviewing (eg Awosunle and Doyle, 2001; Anderson, 1997; Wood, 1997a, b; Ramsey *et al*, 1997).

Last but not least is the move to call centre operations. These currently employ some 400,000 people in the United Kingdom, with a substantial sub-set working in the recruitment field. Working over the telephone to assess potential recruits for clients, these people tend to follow prescribed patterns of questioning for each of their recruitment campaigns. Thus at any one time a dozen or more interviewers may be responding to incoming calls and screening to a common-structured interview pattern. The screening may be on the basis of a number of 'status' variables, reflected in questions such as, 'Do you hold a clean UK driving licence?' Alternatively they may deal directly with competencies such as interpersonal sensitivity, or planning and organising. Sometimes this screening process is followed by more extensive questioning, also conducted by telephone but this time on an 'outbound call' basis. The initial screening interviewer will often have set the appointments for the follow-up interview for those successfully screened. The degree of system necessary in conducting high volume recruitment in this way lends itself very readily to structured interview approaches. There is, in fact, nothing new about the use of screening interviews in high volume situations. Miles *et al* (1946) describe a study in which US Marine Corps recruits were effectively screened for 'neuropsychiatric disability' at a rate of three per minute [*sic*].

SUMMARY

1. Structured interviews vary in form, from simple planning aids to precise prescriptions of questions and admissible responses.

2. A number of forms of structured interview are aimed at gathering clear evidence of behaviour.

3. A variety of methods are available for deriving the dimensions for a structured interview. One of these is the repertory grid in which expert judges reveal the dimensions relevant to their judgements through a simple card-sorting task. Another is the critical incident technique in which subject matter experts (SMEs) are questioned about significant processes. A variety of other job analysis techniques also lead to the specification of relevant behaviour.

4. Competencies are used as the basis for many interviews. A competency is defined as: an underlying characteristic of a person which is causally related to effective or superior performance in a job or role.

5. Criterion-based interviewing is derived from assessment centre technology and involves the systematic exploration of evidence in relation to practically discrete areas of behaviour. Competency-based interviewing is used interchangeably as a term with criterion-based interviewing.

6. Critical incident technique has given rise to the situational interview, in which candidates indicate their responses to hypothetical situations and to the Patterned Behaviour Description Interview (PBDI) in which they are asked about their actual experiences.

7. The Structured Psychometric Interview (SPI) involves the development of questions, the responses to which distinguish between superior and ineffective exponents of a role. The dependence of the technique on precise patterns of language implies that both questions and interpretative frameworks for responses are tightly specified, with implications for training.

8. Research generally shows the predictive superiority of structured over unstructured interviews.

9. Currently a number of forces can be identified that support the increased use of structured interviews.

4

The extended interview

DEGREES OF STRUCTURE

One aspect of selection processes is the idea of taking people through an extended procedure. Such procedures seem often to be based on the idea of making an exacting scrutiny of the candidate and/or the notion of giving a number of interested parties the opportunity for involvement in that scrutiny. Regardless of the degree to which the procedures used are actually made up of interviews as such, a number of organisations refer to them as the extended interview. The term second interview is sometimes used similarly: while a second interview is sometimes simply an interview undergone by those who survived a first interview, and its methods are not defined, in some organisations second interview denotes a different and generally extended process.

As well as assessment centres, as outlined in Chapter 3 and discussed further below, the processes considered here include somewhat less structured but still quite extensive methods. There are sometimes whole days in which groups of interviewers are gathered together to take candidates through a series of separate interviews each to cover at least broadly pre-determined areas. Thus candidates for an engineering post might experience a technical interview from a specialist, a personnel interview from a human resources manager, and then an overall interview from a senior manager. How far the content of such processes is prescribed in advance will vary, but it would be unusual for this to extend to the detailed level of specification set out in the more advanced forms of structured interview as described in Chapter 3. However, because there is some structuring and very often some degree of final discussion about what has gone on, these processes are likely to be somewhat more rigorous than those usually used in conventional selection interviewing.

Relatively little research has been carried out on this class of interview outside the area of assessment centres, which is described in more detail below and which has been subject to prolonged and detailed scrutiny. I have sat in on some of the discussions following these processes, and often the view of one of the interviewing team prevails, and evidence is adduced which was not covered in any form of initial job specification. Again, though, at least this evidence is out in the open when there is such a discussion.

Quite often, additional information such as that provided from psychometric instruments will be considered in discussion together with the interview information. Even so the procedures together are unlikely to represent the levels of rigour and accuracy attained either by structured interviewing or by assessment centres. Having a number of interviewers involved, having them explore more or less prescribed areas and having at least semi-formalised discussion of all the information gathered may help reduce the level of subjectivity somewhat.

THE BOARD OR PANEL INTERVIEW

In the board interview interviewing is carried out by a group of people, typically acting under the chairmanship of one of their number[1]. As with other forms of extended interview process there may be a division of labour, with different people exploring different aspects of the candidate's suitability. This type of interview should be distinguished from a two-person interview, where two interviewers each take on the role of questioner or note-taker. In fact in many panel interviews there may be some degree of control in terms of the chairman allocating time to different interviewers and inviting them in turn to put forward their questions. However, there is typically little or no control over note-taking and there may be little control over the deliberative processes or discussion used to formulate the evaluation of the candidates.

Usually when a board interview has been decided upon there is a strong representational element in those making it up. Thus such

---

[1] The term board is sometimes used in the sense referred to here, but also in the sense of a body responsible for a recruitment and selection process as a whole, as in the Civil Service Selection Board (CSSB). This has sometimes led to confusion, even among researchers, not helped, of course, by the fact that board or panel interviews are among the methods used by such bodies!

processes are frequently used in local government situations where the panel may comprise a mixture of voluntary elected members and salaried officers and where there is a requirement for concerned stake-holders to have a say in the interview process.

In certain medical appointments, a variety of parties is common; doctors, managers, nurses all have their say in the appointment process by sitting on a board or panel. Sometimes these panels are preceded or followed by a so-called informal meeting, not uncommonly dubbed 'trial by sherry'. In every situation the degree of control varies. It cannot be assumed that those interviewing will have had any relevant training and they may only gather together as a body for the purposes of making a particular appointment, with the next appointment to be made requiring in its turn a different group of representatives. Panel members may also turn up or not in a relatively arbitrary way, so that the panel chairperson may not know in advance who will be present.

Despite a certain haphazardness on occasions, in some measure such processes can be seen to be fair. They may have the important advantage of gauging whether the candidate in potentially politi-cally sensitive roles can be seen as sufficiently 'one of us' to be able to be acceptable to the stakeholders present and those whom they may represent. This carries with it the notion that changing the *status quo* may be hard with such methods, almost regardless of what may be in a job description or competency model. It may, by the same token, promote or preserve the exercise of prejudice. Notwithstanding these difficulties Wiesner and Cronshaw's (1988) study showed higher levels of validity even for unstructured board than unstructured individual interviews. Structured board interviews produced validities only slightly lower on average than structured individual interviews.

ASSESSMENT CENTRES

Sometimes what is meant by an extended interview is what would other-wise be described as an assessment centre. The degree of interviewing as such in a centre will vary. It is not too much of a stretch of the imagina-tion to regard the whole process as equivalent to an interview, in that the candidate does have various 'questions' put to him or her, albeit through a variety of exercises.

Assessment centres use simulations of work-like situations in order to produce evidence of a candidate's suitability for roles related to those situations. Assessors are typically trained in some detail in the processes with which they are working and, as indicated in Chapter 3, this is something which will often distinguish the whole use of assessment centre methods from the more conventional interviewing practices. In fact, in best-ordered assessment centres assessors are trained to make distinctions amongst observing behaviour, recording it (typically by making detailed *verbatim* notes if the exercise involves speech), classifying behaviour according to competencies relevant to the role, and finally evaluating it in terms of the strength of the competency indicated (see Figure 4.1). This final evaluation process itself is often two-stage. An initial view is taken by an assessor who has observed a particular exercise but there is considerable discussion and ratification or otherwise of the evaluation level given at the assessor 'washup' meeting. (Indeed the washup session might even be regarded as comprising a series of mini-interviews of assessors by their colleagues as they are asked to support their conclusions.) The British Psychological Society (BPS) currently has a working group

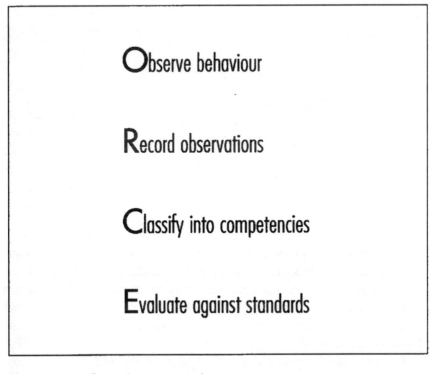

Figure 4.1 *Stepwise process in assessment*

producing a series of guidelines and standards for best practice in assessment centre usage. This initiative follows, though at considerable distance in time, a similar one in the United States. A number of different assessment centre exercise types are described below.

The group discussion

In group discussions candidates are given a single problem or a series of problems to address. Groups vary in size from between four to seven people and the time allowed for discussion will vary typically between 30 minutes and an hour. Group discussions may be assigned role or non-assigned role. In assigned-role group discussions each candidate is given a particular part to play, such as advocacy of one particular site for the location of a new factory. In non-assigned role discussions the group is advised that it is a management team required to consider together some issues of interest to the company as a whole and to come up with recommendations to pass to senior management. Issues discussed may be broad, such as communication strategies or the introduction of total quality management, or they may have a rather more specific agenda of management problems, such as handling the temporary closure of the staff car park.

Analysis exercises

In these exercises the format is usually that of a business case study in which a variety of documents are examined, conclusions are drawn and recommendations made. Candidates will usually work on such an exercise on their own. They may simply submit a written paper or their deliberations may lead to a presentation to a group of assessors.

In-baskets

With in-baskets (or in-trays or in-boxes), the candidate has to cope with a range of correspondence that has accumulated in a predecessor's office. Some of the items may require immediate action. There may be clashes of priorities. There may also be some hidden issues that will only show up as links among items are explored; assessments are based not only on the immediate replies to correspondence items but also on the pattern of future meetings and other activities planned.

Role-plays

A variety of different role-play situations are used in assessment centres. Some of these can be seen as coming close to other types of interview in that an interview format is used. Quite often, the candidate is required to conduct some form of interview with a role-player, typically with an assessor acting as a neutral observer. Common situations used are a sales call, a disciplinary discussion with a subordinate, or an information gathering interview with a third party. Where the role-play approximates closer to other forms of interview is where the meeting is with a supposed senior person in the organisation (see box below).

SOME ROLE-PLAY SITUATIONS

You are a representative for the Greenspace Care Company, a service organisation which supplies and maintains potted plants in offices. You are to meet Jean Morris, office manager for the head office of the South Blankshire Building Society. You have not met Jean before but you understand that she is interested in regular maintenance of plants and the provision of cut flowers for main reception areas, a service that you would have to subcontract.

You are Pat Dawson, factory manager of the East Walton plant of the ACME Fastener Company. You are due to see Lou Smithers, a supervisor who has been the subject of some complaints from other staff members. You have a number of documents relating to the situation, which you must read before meeting Lou in 30 minutes time.

You are Jo(e) Diestrait, a partner in the accountancy firm of Trimble and Trimble. A decision has been taken in principle to merge with another firm, Wily and Dodge. You are to meet Les Marks, one of their partners, to find out more about their internal administrative procedures.

You have just taken over as Assistant Personnel Director (Recruitment) in a large catering company. You have been asked to meet Astrid Starr, non-executive director, who has recently written to the Chairman about the company's record on the employment of disabled people.

In all cases it is the neutral assessor who actually makes the evaluation of behaviour. However, part of the information on which this evaluation is based may come from a mini-interview with the role-player. This is conducted by the assessor after the candidate has left the room, and covers the aspects of the candidate's behaviour which had a negative or a positive impact on the role-player, and a discussion about who appeared to be in charge of the meeting.

Interviews within the assessment centre

Interviews as such and as normally understood do actually take place in assessment centres in a variety of ways. To begin with there is the in-basket interview, frequently but not invariably used to add further information to that given in the written work. This interview is conducted after a preliminary examination of the work that has been done by the candidate. This examination may take anything up to an hour. The assessor prepares and then asks a range of questions designed to follow up further on the work done. For example, if a number of items have been discarded the interview may shed further light on whether this was deliberate, accidental or a result of lack of time. The in-basket interview can also be used to explore specific competencies, just as a criterion-based interview does. For example seeking the candidate's views of the various characters depicted in the in-basket may give clues to their interpersonal judgement. Candidates will sometimes also offer further information about their typical approach to handling issues akin to those depicted in the in-basket.

The criterion-based structured interview discussed in Chapter 3 is, of course, something else which can be included in the assessment centre process. One of the principles in assessment centre design is to have multiple coverage of the competencies and sometimes these may be relatively under-represented in the other exercises. As indicated in Chapter 3 the criterion-based interview may then be used to extend the coverage of competencies. This is illustrated in Figure 4.2. (Note that the coverage of competencies by exercises will vary according to the detailed content as well by type of exercise. Thus Figure 4.2 is not intended to be definitive.)

Usually in assessment centres a further source of information is available to assessors – the participant report. One of these will usually be completed in relation to each exercise undertaken and they serve to supplement the assessor's observations.

EXERCISE/ACTIVITY

Competency	In-basket	Role-play	Competency based interview
Strategic vision	✓✓		✓✓
Understanding complexity	✓✓	✓	
Concern with personal impact	✓	✓✓	✓
Staff development	✓		✓✓
Negotiation	✓	✓✓	✓
Self motivation	✓	✓	✓✓

✓ Some coverage
✓✓ Strong coverage

Figure 4.2 *Competency coverage by exercise type*

FEEDBACK AND FOLLOW-UP INTERVIEWING

When candidates have gone through various forms of extended procedures there is scope to give them feedback on their performance to date. As indicated in Chapter 1 this is quite commonly done in conjunction with psychometric procedures and, indeed, with regard to psychometric instruments it is a principle enshrined in the recommendations of the Institute of Personnel and Development on psychometric use. Giving feedback can also provide an opportunity to gather further information, which may in itself be used to refine the initial interpretation of the candidate's psychometric results. Thus the feedback then incorporates an interview process within it. One commonly asked question during follow-up discussions is whether the results just fed back were in line with expectations and common experience. Where there are discrepancies these may be a matter for further exploration or comment. The box below shows an example of a feedback interview following the administration of a standard psychometric procedure and the relevant passage from a subsequent write-up.

Interviewer: There are several indications from your 16PF results that you are quite independent-minded.

Candidate: Yes, I'd go along with that.

Interviewer: You will probably have some pretty clear views yourself in advance on an issue or problem and you may actually come to conclusions quite quickly.

Candidate: Yes.

Interviewer: Can you think of a time when you have done that?

Candidate: Yes. We had a major re-financing job to do last year on a line of credit required for expansion. I felt we should work with XYZ Bank and I approached them and just one other source, as a sort of benchmark, and then I drove through the choice of XYZ.

Interviewer: Like many people who are independent and quick in their summing up, you may not always see the need to take others along with you. You do not seem to feel a strong need for the support of a group.

Candidate: I'm not so sure about that. I think you have to carry the team along, and I always make a point of consulting with other people.

The candidate shows evidence of elevated independence and also a high level of enthusiasm. She appears quite dominant and will probably seek to impose her position upon others. During feedback she recognised aspects of this style, but felt she adopted a more consultative approach than indicated here. It may be worth exploring further the way in which she has worked with her current subordinates and peers, in terms of team-building.

Reports of feedback interviews can be used to indicate yet further issues for interviewers to explore later on. However, there is a note of caution to be sounded here. While helping the next stage interviewer they may also cue the interviewee in advance. It is necessary, if such approaches are not just to produce contrary evidence at the later stage (ie the interviewee denying or explaining away the difficult behavioural area opened up), for the interviewer to have training in probing in sufficient depth. In the example given above the follow-up interviewer would need to elicit evidence *vis-à-vis* the candidate's team behaviour, not just seek affirmation or denial of support to the team.

Another approach is to reserve feedback until after all processes are complete. This obviates the difficulty just outlined of cueing the candidate, but it does also mean that the maximum value may not have been extracted from the interviewing process. One potential solution to this is to give very strong guidance to interviewers as to specific questions to ask. Such an approach has been developed by the test publishers ASE in relation to follow-up interviewing after applications of the 16 Personality Factor Questionnaire (16PF), a commonly used self-report personality inventory. Questions are provided for a range of different combinations of scores on the various 16PF scales.

WORK SAMPLING INTERVIEWS AND AUDITIONS

Another form of extended process involves the direct sampling of behaviour required in work. The degree to which this can be seen as falling into an interview format as such will vary. Work sampling methods in general require people to reproduce aspects of the work and these may be supplemented by questions. In the theatrical audition the candidate may present a set piece, may be required to read lines from a new script and/or be asked questions about their own work. Often very large numbers of people – perhaps hundreds for a handful of parts – are seen initially and a smaller number called back. In such cases the first session may equate to what, for other jobs, would often be a paper-sifting process. The first of such auditions will necessarily usually be short. When theatrical auditions are held for entry to drama school a fee is usually charged to the candidate, an aspect of the interview process not routinely reproduced elsewhere! This may have the advantage of deterring the frivolous or casual application. It must also defray some of the costs of what is necessarily a labour-intensive process.

Comparable methods are used in other aspects of leisure and entertaining. For instance in the selection of croupiers a second-stage process may follow a short initial interview. In the second stage candidates work at a gaming table alongside fully trained staff and are observed by management and others.

CONCLUSION

There are many strands in the so-called extended interview process. One common thread is a degree of structure. This may at the very least be implied even if there are multiple interviewers, in that each is to some degree given an area to pursue. (However, I know of one situation where 16 people interviewed one particular candidate over a course of two days, and without any structure whatsoever being imposed on any of them!) The scope for pursuit of different areas and the balance of different viewpoints in interpretation may be a reason for the apparent superiority of the unstructured board over the unstructured individual interview. Thus the board interview can scarcely avoid some structure. Certainly without structure there is little guarantee that extended time will be used at all profitably.

SUMMARY

1. Extended or second interview procedures may include a number of activities not necessarily in interview format as such. Assessment centres are sometimes referred to in this way.

2. Board or panel interviews, where a candidate is interviewed by a number of people, may involve a significant element of representation among board members. Research suggests higher validity for these interviews than for unstructured individual interviews.

3. In assessment centres a range of exercises are used and assessors are trained to base their evaluations on behavioural evidence shown in these exercises. Criterion-based interviews may be used in assessment centres, and role-plays may be cast in the form of an interview. Interviews may be used to add to information provided by an in-basket exercise.

4. Giving feedback on a procedure such as a psychometric test may provide an opportunity for a follow-up interview on that procedure.

5. For some jobs candidates are required to reproduce the relevant behaviour directly, as in a theatrical audition.

5

The use of interviews in managing and enhancing performance

INTRODUCTION

The interviews considered in this chapter differ in several ways from those that have been the focus so far. First, they are related to the performance of existing staff as opposed to the selection of new staff. They can involve day-to-day aspects as exemplified in the disciplinary interview. They may also reflect a more forward-looking stance as shown in interviews related to the future development of staff. Sometimes these interviews form part of a developed and integrated system of management. Sometimes, though, they stand apart from other management processes with little or no integration. This may well limit their effectiveness. Thus there may be different terminologies with their own language for describing performance and behaviour, between appraisal and development. These might continue to be used separately or attempts made to translate from one to the other. Either approach could be confusing and dysfunctional. In a more integrated approach, language and standards would be common.

A second difference between interviews discussed in this chapter and those considered earlier is to do with the intended flow of information. As we have seen in selection the main emphasis is typically upon gaining information from the interviewee by use of the interview process. Interviewees clearly draw upon their personal history in making their responses. In the interviews considered here the interviewer gathers and reflects upon information available in advance of the interview and then presents this to the interviewee, albeit for discussion and possible elaboration or amendment (see Figure 5.1). (One variant upon this concept is when the person being interviewed provides their own evaluation of their performance which may then be compared with ratings and other information produced by or available to the interviewer.)

The third difference about the interviews reviewed here, and those examined in earlier chapters, is that they can be seen as aspects of performance management. This has been characterised by Armstrong (1995) as involving 'the joint and continuing review of performance against (agreed) objectives, requirements and plans and the agreement and implementation of improvement and further development plans.'

Interviews, of different sorts and at different stages, are an integral part of any system of performance management, but they are not the whole of it. The formulation and communication of the overall vision and direction of the organisation is another critical, underpinning, part. So too is the actual provision of the development opportunities identified. Closer to the interview itself, and fitting in with the notion raised in Chapter 1 of the interview as merely a specialised form of communication, is the idea of ongoing performance support through discussions and feedback.

APPRAISALS

Who conducts?

These interviews are usually conducted directly by the manager of the person concerned. In other cases they are conducted by a manager two levels up, though quite often in such cases the immediate manager is involved in some form of follow-up discussion.

A recent survey (SHL, 1995) found appraisal by peers being used in 7 per cent of respondent companies but suggested a substantial interest in extending the range of appraisers. It is common for all such interview processes to be subject themselves to further sign-off by another authority. The most common example is when an appraisal conducted by a manager is endorsed and/or annotated by that person's own manager (the 'grandparent'). Sometimes the sign-off process may use a body such as a career management review panel. In such cases information about the person being reported upon may be presented by the appraising manager, who in effect is interviewed by

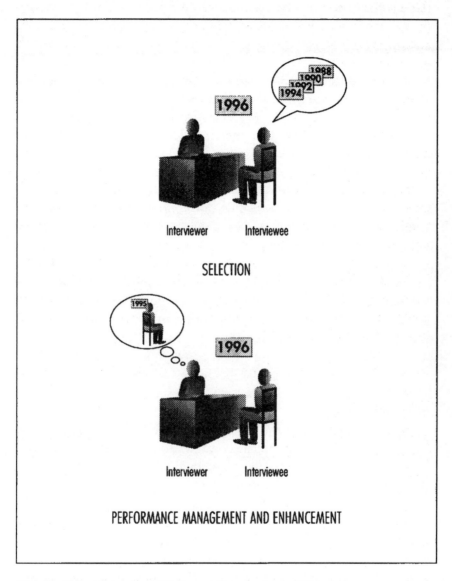

Figure 5.1 *Sources of information in two different interview settings*

the panel on the appraisee's behalf (a situation comparable to that extent to the questioning of an assessor in the assessment centre washup discussion, as referred to in Chapter 4.)

Appraisals and pay

Appraisals have commonly been used with the purpose of reviewing performance over the previous period and setting some standards and objectives for the future. Typically the previous period is a year and very often the appraisals are, accordingly, conducted around the period of the year end.

One of the complications to which this gives rise is that the process inevitably gets bound up with the question of determining pay rises. Much has been said and written on this subject. There is a school of thought (eg Maier, 1958) that says that pay discussions should be entirely separate from appraisal as the former can sometimes take the shape of a negotiating exercise, whereas the latter is intended to be an objective review of what has gone before. In some organisations there is an effective separation of the two, perhaps by a time period as long as a quarter of a year. In other organisations the nettle is firmly grasped and the two are linked together. The SHL survey referred to above revealed that of the one hundred organisations studied 32 per cent reported 'determining salary increase' as one of the objectives of their appraisal scheme; 27 per cent reported no linkage between appraisals and pay.

The complications of the linkage, whatever attempts to separate them, are, of course compounded when ratings of performance are required to be fitted into a given distribution with a direct knock-on effect to pay or even the determination of who should be made redundant. Managers are sometimes required to do this, clearly distorting attempts at objectivity of the process, especially for those managing relatively small groups of people as most managers still do! (While preparing this book I learnt of a well-known organisation who introduced a new appraisal scale while in the middle of a major downsizing operation. Managers were required to use three categories: 'superior', 'satisfactory' and 'should be let go'. One-third of staff were required to be placed in each category. Requests for clarification of the criteria to be used were met with disapproval rather than attempts at enlightenment!)

Appraisals and behaviour

Even in those cases where the link to pay or other decisions is not made directly, there is often a problem of over-generous ratings. This can have a variety of effects. In some cases it results in difficulties if there is a need to discipline or even fire staff. It is quite common, for instance, for someone who is suddenly declared as producing an unsatisfactory performance to have had appraisal ratings, perhaps going back over years, which suggest just the opposite. This tendency to avoid difficult situations in the appraisal interview itself by making inflated ratings can also mean that a number of labels such as 'effective', 'satisfactory', 'to standard' and 'average' are seen as derogatory. This is of course by no means literally the case.

These difficulties seem to persist even when specific behaviours mentioned in appraisals are clearly indicated in what is known as behavioural anchorings. These are meant to show precisely the types of behaviour that would support a rating at the ends of the scale and/or at certain intermediate points. Behaviourally anchored scales do not seem particularly easy to produce, as scales purporting to be designed in this way often fail when tested against the touchstone of adequately indicating behaviour. Thus descriptions such as 'shows excellent knowledge' have a tendency to creep in.

The source of this difficulty may be attributed to a limited understanding of what is meant by behaviour. A useful definition is 'What a person actually says or does or does not say or do when required to do so.' The emphasis is clearly upon what is observable, what has actually happened. The use of this idea in appraisal interviewing is akin to that in criterion-based interviewing, in particular in selection (see Chapter 3).

Another process which sometimes happens in appraisal situations is that the official scales become littered with the grace notes of pluses, minuses and other shadings. This again detracts from the behavioural anchoring and the clarity that that is intended to introduce, and is also likely to mean that, in effect, no two managers actually rate in the same way. Thus any of these limitations in the design or application of what is meant to be a systematic process can adversely affect the appraisal interview.

Appraisal training

The way round some of these difficulties is, as with so many other things, partly through effective training. A process such as behavioural anchoring is unlikely to be effectively understood and taken on board through simply distributing documentation, although this is often the approach taken. The basis of any training will be to instil in the minds of those conducting the appraisal that they need to go through a stepped process. As with other processes inherently based on behaviour, it is behavioural evidence that is likely to stand up best in the appraisal interview and this should be to hand. An appraisal training programme is set out below, followed by a model approach to conducting an appraisal, such as can be found in the documentation used by many personnel departments. There is considerable emphasis upon gaining buy-in to the points being made, and to the process being one of joint discussion.

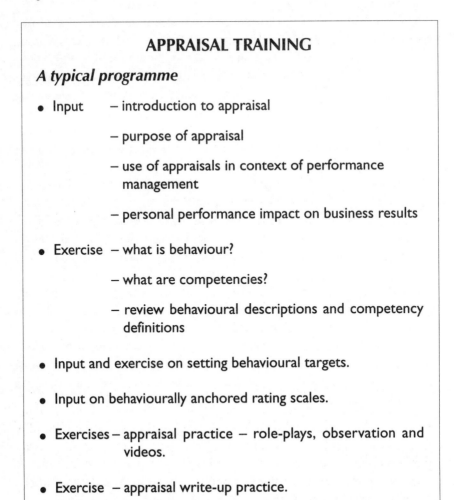

APPRAISAL TRAINING

A typical programme

- Input — introduction to appraisal

    — purpose of appraisal

    — use of appraisals in context of performance management

    — personal performance impact on business results

- Exercise — what is behaviour?

    — what are competencies?

    — review behavioural descriptions and competency definitions

- Input and exercise on setting behavioural targets.

- Input on behaviourally anchored rating scales.

- Exercises — appraisal practice — role-plays, observation and videos.

- Exercise — appraisal write-up practice.

A 'model' appraisal process

Beginning of year – objectives set and clarified in discussions between appraiser and appraisee.

Ongoing through year:

- gathering of performance data

- routine feedback on performance

One month before appraisal meeting – date set.

Appraisal interview
- Review of work including successes and areas for improvement.

- Consideration of special circumstances or constraints placing limitations on performance.

- Review of job description/responsibilities as appropriate.

- Discussion of professional or managerial development needs.

- Identification of targets for development.

- Setting of objectives.

Appraisal write up
- Within two weeks of meeting.

- Space for comment by appraisee.

- Review by appraiser's boss (grandparent).

Increasingly, appraisal systems are linked to competencies so that these provide the model used to describe behaviour. It is also, perhaps, commonplace that appraisals themselves are something of a Cinderella activity in many organisations. The existence of an overall performance management framework of which competencies form a part may reinforce better use of appraisals and as indicated are likely to be an integral part of training.

Apart from the problems already discussed, it is not unusual for appraisals to be conducted late or not at all. The SHL appraisal survey (1995) indicated that many appraisers – 44 per cent – receive no training even though only 6 per cent of organisations reported providing no training.

McGregor (1957) realised the limitations in the practice of appraisal when he urged a move from what he saw as a focus on determination of weaknesses to a concentration on performance and on the behaviour necessary to promote effective performance. This coaching stance can be seen as a key part of the more broadly-based performance management which, at least in intention, distinguishes today's from yesterday's approach to managing the human resource.

Armstrong (1995) attributes much of the failure of traditional appraisal schemes to the tendency to make them form-filling exercises, with an emphasis on centrally held records, rather than as notation relating to a worthwhile interview process and something to be used to support continued interaction and discussion throughout the year.

One specific approach possible in appraisal interviewing, though one not apparently widely employed, is that of rank ordering strengths on the various competencies covered. Thus the appraisee is not faced with ratings on an absolute scale or one fixed by reference to a peer group but rather is provided with information reflecting relative performance one to another of the different areas rated. This does, of course, have a disadvantage where the appraisal is to be linked to reward. Its advantage would seem to be its 'non-destructive' nature (cf a similar argument by Fox (1996), with respect to psychometric measures of ability).

PERFORMANCE IMPROVEMENT AND DISCIPLINARY INTERVIEWS

Underperformance

Interviews relating to underperformance mix two strands. One is the exploration of information and, associated with that, the setting of standards for the future. The other is the need to maintain a legitimate disciplinary line with the individual concerned. The first of these purposes is something that could be regarded as comparable to the appraisal process. The second, though, can conflict with this and the stating of problems part of the interview may in itself make either party ill-placed to consider a positive way forward. To begin with, conflict between the two parties involved may arise as a result of the discussion unless it is handled with extreme care. As the interviewer may feel himself on the same occasion to be an aggrieved party this may be problematic. If the person being interviewed feels that this is the first time that the expectations now being aired as unfulfilled are being made clear, they too are likely to feel upset.

There will also be pressure on the interviewer to make the discussion as short as possible, both to reduce discomfort and to ensure that what has been said can clearly be noted for the record. In some cases it may be an effective tactic to split the interview in two; the what is wrong part, and the way forward part. Both may then be addressed in a calmer atmosphere.

Of course prevention is better than cure. In an atmosphere in which feedback is given and accepted on a continuing basis in a series of interviews throughout the year the need for the disciplinary interview as such is far less likely to arise. Thus in environments characterised by ongoing performance management, positive and negative aspects of performance are routinely discussed.

Gross misconduct

Disciplinary interviews relating to gross misconduct are, for the moment, separated out from other forms of performance-improvement interviews. However, note that the differences are not absolute. In some cases, such as theft, the interview is seen merely as a formal necessity prior to dismissal, but in others there is a potential continuum with other aspects of performance-improvement interviewing. Thus issues of poor time keeping or apparent incapacity to deliver work effectively will in some cases result in the type of performance-improvement interactions discussed above. Some of these may be entirely supportive, but others may fall in effect into the gross misconduct category. What judgement is made of the starting point may depend on the views of the manager or, indeed, the impact upon a third party. A minor error which results in the loss to an organisation of a million pound order is likely to be seen as more serious than the same error picked up before it issues in such a disaster. A disciplinary interview is likely to concentrate on procedures and facts. In some cases the interviewee will have the right to have a trade union or other representative present.

STAFF DEVELOPMENT

Development centres

Development centres use the methodology discussed under extended interviews in Chapter 4, but for purposes of staff development. The same assessment processes typically apply. However, feedback is usually more detailed and participants may be given a variety of further self-discovery tasks to do, as well as detailed instruction in the method of assessment being used.

The assessor has several different tasks to accomplish in feedback. He needs to present clearly the information and the ratings to which it leads. Sometimes it may be appropriate to talk primarily in terms of performance on an exercise-by-exercise basis, while in other cases feedback will need to reflect the results on a competency basis. For the centre participant whose results are summarised in Figure 5.2 there is more consistency of performance within exercises than within competencies, so feedback would generally be conducted on the basis of each exercise in turn.

It is particularly important not to get involved in a negotiation on the ratings given but to represent these clearly as the combined opinion of the assessing team. The way to do this is to present the evidence – that is, the observed behaviour – first, followed by the evaluation. If the evaluation is given first this tends to result in defensiveness on the part of the centre participant (the interviewee). By presenting the behavioural evidence first the evaluation given is seen to come naturally, arising logically from what has been presented. In the same way it is not usually a good idea, when giving development-centre feedback, to ask participants what they thought of their performance in a particular exercise, or in relation to a particular competency. If the participant's view does not accord with the assessor's this advance declaration of a position may lead to defensiveness and difficulty in accepting the evidence.

If the feedback interview is to be most effective and worth while, careful preparation of the participant is necessary. This will include detailed familiarisation with the centre processes – how the observations are made and how evidence is pooled among assessors. The necessary training and briefing for this will often be undertaken during the centre itself while the assessors are holding their deliberations.

EXERCISE

Competency	In-basket	Analysis	Role-play	Group discussion
Strategic vision	TS	DN		TS
Understanding complexity	TS	DN	DN	
Concern with personal impact	DN	DN	DN	S
Staff development	TS			TS
Negotiation	TS		DN	S
Self motivation	DN	DN	TS	TS

DN   Development Need
TS   To Required Standard
S   Strength

Figure 5.2 *Development centre, summary results*

For participants to receive feedback, they need some explanation and understanding of the competencies. Sometimes briefing on this is undertaken in advance of the centre and this may be particularly so where competencies are common between centre processes and others. In other cases the briefing on competencies is given on the centre itself, while the assessors are undertaking their discussions. The feedback itself may extend to discussion of possible career options and the implications of those. Part of a development-centre feedback interview is shown overleaf.

DEVELOPMENT-CENTRE FEEDBACK INTERVIEW

Assessor: Jack   *Participant*: Tim

Jack: Well, as you will know by now I'm here to take you through the results of our observations over the last two days. All the assessors have had a lengthy discussion about all the participants. You know from the in-basket interview that I studied your work on that exercise, but I'm not just reporting on that. I'm going to tell you about the other exercises, too, so what I'm telling you about is the combined view of everyone. Is that clear?

Tim: Yes, that's okay.

Jack: You've seen the competency model and understand the terms used in that and you've also had a look at the whole assessment process that we are using?

Tim: Yes, I'm fairly clear about all that.

Jack: Well, I'm going to begin by talking about the competency called strategic vision. That's the one to do with indicating how far you would have what's sometimes called a 'helicopter view' of the world of the business.

Tim: Yes, I was rather intrigued by that one particularly because I wasn't at all sure how you could possibly find that out from the exercises that we did.

Jack: Well, it will come out to different degrees in each of the exercises. Let's start with the group discussion exercise. You were all working on that problem of the site for the new administrative offices to support the three factories. Your preliminary work had shown that you had paid some attention to the costs and you spoke about those quite a lot during the discussion.

Tim: Yes.

Jack: Now, you did follow on when Ranjit raised a question of the long-term future of the business to say that your cost model might well vary if, as he was suggesting, one of the factories was actually closed down, so you were able to identify with a different future and that's one of the things that we looked for. However, you didn't indicate that you had thought of that in advance. It wasn't in your notes and you actually said, 'Well if that is a possible scenario . . .'. You also disagreed with Jennifer when she said that it would be important to consider different patterns of working in the future with a lot more people being likely to do their administrative work from home.

Tim: Yes, I remember that. I was really impatient at that point because we only had ten minutes left and we had spent a lot of time talking about process.

Jack: Yes, a lot of the discussion did go on that. Of course one way of moving that along would have been for someone earlier – and it could have been you as well as anybody else – to have raised the question of longer term objectives and the need to consider the future shape of the business within the process for managing the discussion. That could well have had an impact on the approach taken.

Tim: I'm not sure, though, that it's really fair to think of that exercise as something that would really have got us on to a strategic approach. After all, we all knew that we had to get in our three-pennyworth somewhere and there was a jostling for position and people were trying to make sure they stated their views rather than it being set out as something with a very long-term horizon.

Jack: Certainly if someone didn't, as you say, get their three-pennyworth in and contribute at all to the discussion there wouldn't have been any behaviour to observe. However, if the view that you had wanted to put forward had been a strategic one then that's where you would have chosen to, as it were, spend your three-pennyworth.

Tim: Well, I can't deny the behaviour as you have presented it and I see how it could have been slanted differently though I must confess that I hadn't seen that at the time and I still would not have thought it was the exercise best calculated to produce that evidence.

Jack: Well okay, on the basis of what we did see here, though, this performance would not have evidenced behaviour to the standard required of a senior manager in the company with regard to strategic vision and so this would show as a development need.

Tim: Okay well I – yes I can accept that for the moment.

Jack: If we move on to the individual analysis exercise you will remember one of the issues put to you was the marketing implications of a much more integrated relationship with suppliers.

Tim: Yes, I felt more comfortable with that because there were a number of echoes of work I'd done previously in total quality management and I pulled some of that experience out in what I wrote.

Jack: In fact there was a lot of evidence of your thinking at a quite high level and you did refer to total quality. You suggested that there would be a need to see if that could potentially run counter to or alternatively be complementary to those initiatives – I'm quoting directly from your work here. This showed evidence of a clear approach to the analytical aspect of strategic vision. You actually took that further to work through some of the impact upon customers and followed up with the idea of putting yourselves and your suppliers in a further partnership relationship with the customer base.

There was also evidence later in the paper you prepared when you looked at potential risks, that you had quite a grasp on the possibly changing business situation in terms of ultimate customer usage of the product. However, there was little acknowledgement of the impact of all this on people. There had been a clue to this in the briefing notes, but you really didn't do much more than acknowledge that there would be some people impact. You didn't talk further about the effects of changing work patterns and skill mixes.

Tim: Well, I'm not a personnel specialist and I suppose I would have been relying on someone of that sort to pick up that aspect for me.

Jack: In strategic vision, though, we would actually want to see a clearer intention of someone setting such an initiative in motion even if they did involve another individual or specialist group.

Tim: Okay.

Jack: On that basis the picture of this exercise altogether is that this is a competency that was demonstrated to standard but it probably would have come out as a clear strength, that is above the standard basically required, if there had been some further work on the personnel side.

Sometimes the work with the participants goes on to a stage in which they produce detailed recommendations for their own further development action. This may then be the subject of a three-way interview involving their direct manager, who probably would not have been present at the development centre, and a representative of the training and personnel function. In such a follow-up interview there would likely to be detailed discussion of their expectations and requirements for the future.

It may well be that first the assessors and then subsequently the reviewing management team will have at their disposal other information about the interviewee to inform their discussion, such as self-completion questionnaires on future career direction.

Other staff development interviews

In some cases interviews are designed specifically to explore the future interests of staff members and how they see their careers as developing. This may also give an opportunity to look at areas where there may be performance issues requiring resolution. However, the main aim of such interviews is meant to be forward looking rather than having the largely backward-looking focus of the appraisal system. Such interviews may be conducted by staff other than those routinely involved in appraisal interviewing. Thus they may include personnel or HR staff with a special responsibility for development or career planing. Sometimes, again, such interviews are supported by documentation with a variety of questionnaires often being used in advance.

They may also merge into the field of counselling, which is the subject of the next chapter. How far the interviews considered here can be seen as separate from counselling as such will depend on a number of factors. These include the relationship of the interview to the business purposes of the organisation. In these interviews the purposes will be business-led. The link to the business in the case of counselling interviews is likely to be less distinct and may even be consciously separated further. Also the role of the person conducting the interview will be important. In these staff development interviews the interviewer, if not the person's immediate manager is, nevertheless, likely to have some input into decisions about development; questions of resources or money for training courses, for example. Such interviews may also take as a starting point the output from development centres or other processes which include assessment. A sample staff development interview programme is set out below.

Staff development interview programme

Before interview
- Interviewer reviews outputs from other sources (eg development centre, appraisal, career influences questionnaire, psychometric battery).

Interview
- Interviewer asks pre-set questions *and* probes for further understanding.

- Interview concludes with summary of understanding and action plans for interviewee and interviewer.

After interview
- Action plans written up by interviewee.

Ongoing
- Interviewer and interviewee check on actions involving other parties (eg opportunities for job shadowing, course availability).

After interval
- Follow-up meeting – status of plans reviewed.

SUMMARY

1. Interviews used in managing and enhancing performance are directed at *existing* staff. They typically utilise information already gathered rather than using the interview primarily as an information-gathering exercise.

2. Appraisals involve a retrospective examination of performance. They often become bound up with pay reviews. Behaviourally anchored scales help clarify ratings in appraisals. Training in appraisal processes can underpin more objective use of appraisal systems.

3. An ongoing focus on performance with continuing reviews may preclude the need for disciplinary interviews as such. Disciplinary interviews can be seen as one extreme of performance management interviews.

4. In development centres the feedback interview is seen as pivotal in setting performance enhancement in train.

5. Staff development interviews may be conducted by specialised staff with particular responsibility for development and/or career planning. Such interviews will seek to link individual development to specific business goals and outcomes.

6

Interviews in counselling and guidance

INTRODUCTION

Purposes

Interviews used in counselling may have a number of purposes, ranging from situations involving crises such as loss or bereavement, to helping individuals cope with problems or issues requiring resolution, such as initial choice of career or a new career direction[1]. Although the interview is not the only mechanism used in counselling situations it is central and it would be difficult to conceive of counselling taking place which does not involve direct spoken interaction between people. Most often this is between two people but there are also applications of group counselling, with one or more counsellors working with groups of anything from four to sixteen people. One counsellor to two clients is, of course, a very common situation in marriage counselling.

Dictionaries tend to emphasise or confine themselves to the guidance aspect when defining counselling (eg 'to give advice or counsel to, to advise', Baker, 1949). For most professional writers on counselling guidance is seen as a phase or step at most and not the prime purpose. In fact the purpose is more usually described in terms such as enabling the counsellee to understand and to come to terms with the path that he or she should pursue, seeing issues and problems in a

---

[1] Names and addresses of several organisations in the UK that are involved in counselling are given in Appendix II.

perspective beyond the immediate and in the context wider than implied by directly pressing issues and problems. For instance Burnett (1977) defines it as 'a process of interaction between two individuals – the counsellor and the client – the purpose of which is to enable the client to reach a decision on a personal matter such as choosing a career or a job, or to work through a personal difficulty.' Walmsley (1994) summarises the purpose succinctly as 'to help someone help themselves'.

In its *Code of Ethics and Practice for Counsellors* the British Association for Counselling makes a distinction between 'counselling' and the 'use of counselling skills'. The former term is reserved for those situations in which two parties agree to enter into a counselling relationship as such. The latter would apply when a manager with counselling skills may use these as part of routine interactions with staff, for example in connection with performance management as outlined in Chapter 5.

The general form of counselling

Characteristic of many counselling situations is that the emotional aspects are likely to be significant. The issues faced by the person receiving counselling are unlikely to be capable of immediate remedy through the strictly rational process of questioning that would characterise many of the other forms of interviews.

One of the things that is stressed in most writings on counselling is the stepped and unfolding nature of the process. In general this applies both to counselling of an essentially therapeutic nature (see for example Rogers, 1942) and that exercised within a work organisation (see Sworder, 1977). This inevitably means that the process is somewhat extended in time. The most extreme forms of counselling, characterised by psychoanalysis, have procedures which last over periods of years. Dryden and Feltham define 'brief counselling' as lasting from one to twenty sessions; even this may take several months. Most counselling situations that arise in relation to work, whether crisis-based or not, still extend over a period of weeks or months. In redundancy counselling a counsellor tends to remain in contact with the counsellee at least until a new job has been found, or another mode of occupation such as self-employment, arrived at.

In selection interviewing the aim is for the interviewer to extract information so that he can come to a decision, and a secondary aim (if at all) is to provide information to the interviewee. In counselling situations the focus is upon counsellees understanding the information about themselves that is likely to be at their disposal. To this may be added, particularly in redundancy situations, information from the counsellor about the job market, opportunities for training and so on, but these are essentially secondary to the processes of self-discovery (see Figure 6.1).

The form of questioning would be different in counselling. Particularly, but not exclusively, in counselling related to crisis there will be an emphasis on feelings; it is important to understand these and set them in a context, but not to neutralise them entirely. Thus questions designed to elicit feelings – 'How do you feel about that?', 'What was your reaction to that?' – will be a common part of the toolkit of the counselling interviewer, who will also need to ask questions of fact to establish what has actually gone on.

Rogers, in various writings (eg 1961, 1965) placed considerable emphasis upon what he labelled non-directive counselling, again underlining the difference between a heavily guided approach and one in which the counsellor provides the opportunity for the client or counsellee to make his or her own explorations. He characterised (Rogers, 1942) the non-directive viewpoint as placing 'a high value on the right of every individual to be psychologically independent, and maintain his psychological integrity.' By contrast in the directive approach the focus is on 'social conformity and the right of the more able to direct the less able.'

Research quoted by Rogers shows some quite drastic differences in behaviour between counsellors categorised as either non-directive, or directive. For instance the latter spoke much more in counselling sessions. (The extreme members of two such contrasted groups varied by a ratio of 25:1 in this regard.) Directive counsellors were found to ask many specific questions, to state their own views and readily make proposals for action. By contrast the non-directive counsellors spent far more time restating (ie reflecting) what the client had said and giving the client the opportunity to express feelings. Although these differences appear quite marked from the outside it is also reported that the directive counsellors did not recognise that they had taken a distinct lead. Thus in carrying out counselling one's own approach may not be self-evident, and to adopt one or other style routinely may itself require considerable training, practice and reflection.

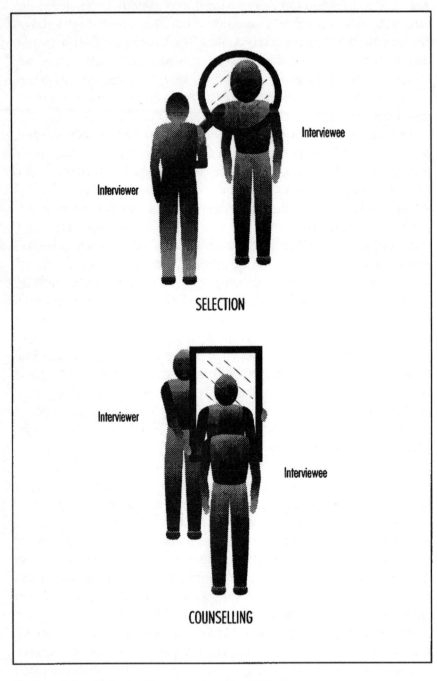

Figure 6.1 *Other's discovery and self-discovery*

The choice between the directive and non-directive approach may reflect the counsellor's value system. It may also reflect sheer force of circumstances. The counsellor dealing with large numbers of redundant staff, with a limited number of sessions booked and aware of certain windows of opportunity closing, may be inclined to be directive at an earlier point than if faced with a potential returnee to full-time work, or someone contemplating a two-year time horizon.

Another way in which the interaction between counsellor and counsellee can be understood is by thinking of it as a working relationship, whereas in a selection interview, of whatever type, the working relationship has yet to start.

There are many books relating to the different issues that can be the subject of counselling: for example Wallbank's *The Empty Bed* (1992) deals particularly with the sexual dimension of bereavement. Some counsellors will recommend publications to a person being counselled and use this as a means of opening up certain areas of discussion. Others may feel that this smacks of a do-it-yourself approach which could compromise the effectiveness of their interactions. However, those being counselled may, in any case, find their way to these books and themselves raise issues set out in them in connection with their own situation. Books may also help in the decision as to whether or not to take up an opportunity for counselling. For example Gough's *Couples in Counselling* (1989) is subtitled, *A consumer's guide to marriage counselling*. It seeks to help people understand what is involved in marriage counselling and whether it may be worthwhile for them.

REDUNDANCY COUNSELLING

Redundancy counselling has become something of an industry in recent years with a variety of specialised firms setting up in this area. It is often argued that it is more appropriate for an external organisation to take on this role than for it to be conducted internally. There are several reasons for this.

It may well be that in times of major change and reorganisation, such as characterise many redundancy situations, the natural support mechanisms that would at other times be in place have gone. For instance, in situations involving mergers between companies, those charged one day with making staff redundant may be looking over their shoulders to see if it will be their turn next. It is also common for a considerable degree of hostility to surround the situation and this may complicate the provision of counselling services internally. Where external firms are used a sum of money is often made available for this purpose and ringfenced from other aspects of the termination package to encourage its use. Concerns about confidentiality may also be more apparent with internal rather than external counselling support.

Some organisations have, though, successfully gone down the route of relying exclusively or largely upon internal counselling support. When they have done so this has typically involved the use of staff somewhat separated from the immediate focus of redundancy. Although these people may not be themselves overly secure, there is scope to see them as standing apart from the immediate decisions and perhaps even the immediate turmoil of change in one particular part of the organisation. In some cases this may be seen as a way of making effective use of personnel or other staff whose roles themselves may have changed.

Whether the counselling interviews and other interventions are conducted internally or externally, a common process is usually adopted. As indicated above this tends to be a stepped programme. It may start with support for the person making others redundant, and continue until the redundant person has found another occupation. A sample programme involving the use of an external consultancy organisation is set out in Figure 6.2.

It can be seen that one-to-one interview sessions form an ongoing part of this process, interwoven with other activities.

As the counselling process progresses the interviews move steadily in the direction of guidance, ultimately taking the form, in effect, of the counsellee checking in with the counsellor and perhaps updating the counsellor on how the latest external selection interview had gone. The counselling interactions may also take place in an environment where there is ready access to sources of information about jobs. Other support mechanisms provided in the same context may include telephone and secretarial services to facilitate the pursuit of job opportunities, as well as advertised and unadvertised vacancies being easily accessible through research facilities.

In the earlier stages of exploration, a number of supportive tools are likely to be used. Some of these will be self-reflection devices

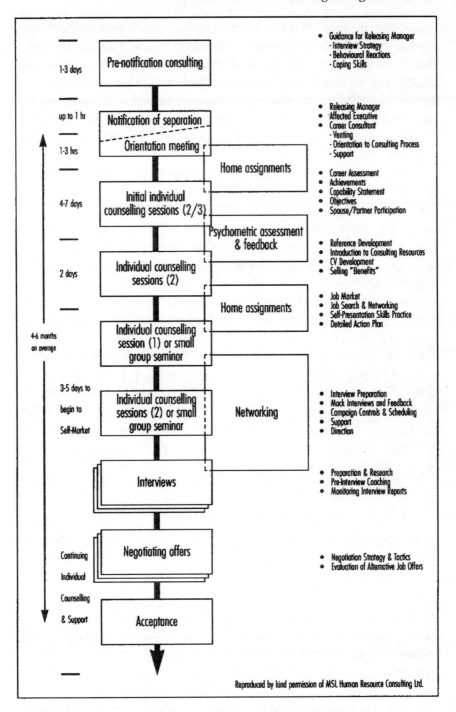

Figure 6.2 *Stepwise programme of redundancy support*

where people may list their achievements and interests, their transferable skills and their strengths. Others may be more formal psychometric instruments such as personality measures. Sometimes, of course, the counsellor will have the requisite skills to deal with the latter. In other circumstances counsellors may use a psychologist or other consultant to support this aspect of their work. What is needed is a counsellor who essentially maintains control of the thread of the communication with the counsellee throughout. Among other things this may involve determining if a particular external intervention is appropriate.

Very often in counselling in relation to redundancy there will be issues that are not immediately on the surface. It is part of the counsellor's role to explore things with the counsellee, giving him or her the scope to understand and express views. Some of this may be painful at times and require admitting to failings or limitations.

There was for some time a theory in counselling that it was particularly irritating individuals who were made redundant, regardless of circumstances: the so-called oyster hypothesis. This view has itself been challenged in some work by Brindle (1992). Using self-report personality questionnaires he examined personalities of senior executives who had been made redundant. He found these people to be more introverted, astute and anxious than an average group of executives, suggesting a tendency for a lower rather than a higher profile.

But regardless of overall or average findings, counsellors have to deal with the particular person before them, warts and all. Getting people to recognise they may be displaying inappropriate interpersonal behaviour – such as being abrasive, or apprehensive – can be problematic. Such behaviour might well pose barriers in the counselling situation itself and it might well be dysfunctional in relation to future jobs. Displays of negativity or lack of interest in a new role may, in particular, strike a wrong note with the recruiting organisation. (The relation between negative statements and a variety of negative outcomes has been studied in a number of ways. For instance Peterson and Seligman (1988) analysed the content of press quotes from members of America's Baseball Hall of Fame over a 50-year period. Pessimistic comments correlated with a shorter life span.) In any of these circumstances the counsellor may reflect back to the counsellee some of the feelings and ideas that had been expressed in order to show these in context. An illustration of this is given below.

Client: And that's what I felt was so unfair. I had been given another group of people to manage and nobody had bothered to explain to them what was happening or how things were changing. They were naturally quite demotivated and took up a lot of my time, which meant I never really got on top of my own group.

Counsellor: So you were upset because the situation your company placed you in made it impossible for you to succeed?

Client: Yes, and so they got rid of me, which as I say was unfair. It's made me realise that before I go into another big management post I need to be very sure what I'm letting myself in for.

Counsellor: So you would feel wary about another role with much staff-management responsibility.

Client: Too right.

Counsellor: Well, your feelings are quite understandable in the light of the experiences you have had.

Client: Yes, I just don't want to be caught out like that again.

Counsellor: You might like to think, though, how far and perhaps when you should voice your concerns to a potential new employer.

Client: How do you mean?

Counsellor: Well, if you voice your concerns at an early stage of discussions with a new company you may find that you give them the impression that you aren't interested. Even if ultimately you decide you are not you might find it helpful, say, in your discussions with other companies to be able to say that company X is still an iron in the fire.

Client: I see what you mean.

Here the counsellor has moved from a non-directive to a directive style. Although the client's behaviour cannot be guaranteed it seems more likely that the direction will be accepted and followed given the clear acknowledgement early on of circumstances and the feelings attached to them.

VOCATIONAL GUIDANCE

There are overlaps between vocational guidance and redundancy counselling, as both may be concerned with the question of career steps.
However, much of vocational guidance interviewing takes place inde-
pendently of the crisis of redundancy. Often it will be undertaken at a
much earlier age and, again, there are various specialist bodies and
agencies working with young people and others in this field.

Very often some form of psychometric tool is used to support these
activities; this has been the case since the earliest days of vocational
guidance. When the National Institute of Industrial Psychology
(NIIP) first provided vocational guidance in 1921 it placed special
emphasis upon the development of an appropriate battery of tests.
(For an account of this see Frisby, 1971.)

Vocational guidance interviewing tends to centre on two questions:

1.   What skills and capabilities does the interviewee possess?
2.   What are the interests and inclinations of the interviewee?

Both of these can be addressed through interviewing but both are
likely to be supported by ability or interest instruments, such as the
Strong-Campbell Interest Inventory (see Campbell, 1974). These will
then tend to form a basis for an informed discussion about possibilities. In this the interviewer may need to get beyond the surface issues
of an interest presenting itself and establish how well founded that
interest is. One of the interviewing approaches used here is to explore
the amount of information that the interviewee has in advance about
the role or roles concerned. When high, this is taken as a positive sign
of interest and likely commitment to the area. This approach has also
been captured in a paper and pencil instrument known as the Job
Knowledge Index (JKI: Kirton, 1976). This provides scales for a
range of different occupations.

The field of vocational guidance, perhaps like that of selection
interviewing, is complicated to some degree by the fact of organisations wishing to present themselves in a positive light. In a research
programme with a leading public company I found that a number of
graduates who had joined felt that they had been misled by the glossy
publicity literature that had been put out by the company in advance.
They indicated that much of the staff turnover among their peers had
been due to a failure of expectations. Sometimes it would be up to the
vocational guidance interviewer, in fact, to point out what may seem

very self-evident but which could be missed. For instance, North Sea divers work for a lot of their time under water in a dark environment; people working in meat packing will have to handle carcasses and various parts of remains of animals to a degree that is unlikely to be familiar to them from their perusal of supermarket chillers or butcher's shop windows.

Personality instruments can also give indications on preferences and so suggest which occupations might and which might not fit the person concerned. For example someone who appeared to be averse to getting involved in persuading others would be unlikely to find a sales role congenial. Someone with a tendency to experiment might fit in well with a product design team. In fact some personality instruments, such as Cattell's 16 Personality Factor Questionnaire (16PF), can give quite direct indications of fit to a range of jobs (see Krug, 1981).

Perhaps one of the most common besetting problems of the vocational guidance interviewer is the interviewee, often but not always a young person, who expects to be told about the things that they might want to do. Couple this with some degree of resentment against authority, and the problem can become magnified. Again, processes of reflecting ideas back to the interviewee are likely to be important and, again, it may take a number of sessions, perhaps involving interested parties such as teachers and parents. An example of a vocational guidance session is given below.

Counsellor: Okay, John. What I see us doing in these sessions is exploring some of the things that might suit you as a career so that you can decide what possibilities you might want to take up. Is that okay?

John: Oh, well I thought you were going to tell me about the courses.

Counsellor: What courses?

John: Well, I don't know do I? But I haven't got any qualifications and my mum says I'll have to go to night school now if I want to get a decent job.

Counsellor: How do you feel about going to night school or evening classes?

John: I don't know. I've got this job in a warehouse just now and it finishes quite early but I'm dead knackered at the end of the day so I don't know about going out and like studying every night.

Counsellor: Well, it certainly wouldn't be every night and how many it was would depend on just what you wanted to do. Did you have any ideas earlier on, before you actually left school?

John: Yeah, well, I wanted to be a professional footballer but my dad was dead against it. I used to play a lot for all different teams when I was at school. I never bothered with exams and that. Anyway, at the end of the day, I couldn't even get a trial. Said I've got to wait another six months. That's why I went into the warehouse. It's a bit boring, but the money's not bad.

Counsellor: So, do you feel like waiting till the end of the six months and have a go at the football, or do you really want to think about other possibilities?

John: I don't know really. My dad said you'd be able to tell me what I ought to do.

By this stage the counsellor has made some discoveries about John, in terms of his interest in football and his wariness about 'night school'. He has probably got some way to go yet before John begins to accept responsibility for his own decisions. On the face of it academic study, especially when he is 'knackered', seems unlikely to suit John, but really the interview so far has only raised questions and hypotheses for further exploration. Is the footballing career just a schoolboy fantasy? If John recognises it as such would he knuckle down to some sort of study course, day-release possibly, if not evening classes? A session with his parents might establish how much influence they had and how far they were prepared to let their son make his own decisions.

OTHER CRISIS COUNSELLING

Just what constitutes a crisis and what form of counselling interviewing might be required will vary from individual to individual and case to case. It is commonplace that in the minor difficulties of everyday life, to have someone else to share the problem is a way of halving that problem. Very often the second party acts mostly as a listening ear and might not offer any specific support or guidance. Given, though, the increasing literature on the question of stress in the workplace (see for example Warr (1987), Firth-Cozens and Handy (1992)) and the evident way in which even such informal offloading can assist, it is perhaps surprising that more widespread use is not made of more fully established and formalised counselling in the workplace. The John Lewis Partnership is one of those that has established counselling as a routine provision at work.

Some commercial organisations provide counselling support in relation to rather specific and perhaps dramatic crisis situations. For instance, a number of building societies and other financial institutions have embarked upon the use of post-incident trauma counselling for those who have experienced armed robberies or hostage abductions. Again there are some specialist firms working in this field. Some of this work involves one-to-one interview counselling. There are also group discussions with a lead facilitator, with considerable emphasis being placed – as with the initial phases of redundancy counselling – on getting the feelings out in the open. Part of the process is focused on helping victims cope with their experience by understanding the pattern of likely stress reactions. This includes anticipation of those negative reactions that might arise in the future as well as reassurance about the likely path to full recovery. The arrangements for this type of support may also include hot-line facilities so that those involved can be given rapid reassurance that help is at hand.

Police, fire services and the military have also in recent years recognised the value of counselling interviewing and, indeed, their work in this field pre-dates the provision of trauma counselling in commercial organisations. Some voluntary aid organisations also use interventions of this type in relation to traumas associated with war conditions and refugee status. Among those working with traumatised children in Rwanda, for instance, unlocking emotions is sometimes facilitated by getting the child to produce a drawing depicting the traumatic event.

Perhaps more systematised historically, and certainly more familiar to many, will be the counselling interviews undertaken in relation to marriage guidance and bereavement, to which we now turn.

MARRIAGE GUIDANCE AND BEREAVEMENT

Marriage guidance

In marriage guidance the interviewer may deal with the parties individually but the greatest value of the intervention is likely to accrue from a joint interview. This can pose considerable demands upon the interviewer. As he or she seeks to establish some initial facts and the current level of feelings in the two parties these feelings themselves are likely to manifest themselves not uncommonly in displays of hostility. This is illustrated below.

Counsellor: So, would you like to tell me about why you've come here today?

Woman: Well, it's him and his unreasonable behaviour, isn't it?

Man: I'm not here to have a quarrel but that's a little rich coming from you.

Woman: You were the one who locked up my cheque book.

Man: It was the only way to stop you spending money we didn't have.

The counsellor's next intervention may well involve an attempt to lay down some ground rules to help establish facts, though at some stage the feelings and emotions will have to be explored.

However, the marriage guidance interviewer fairly regularly spots a particular point of friction and begins to point the way to a possible resolution, so heading off the potential marriage breakdown. Such a case is also illustrated.

Man: And we don't now ever seem to dicuss problems together.

Woman: But that's because if I say anything you just say I'm moaning and you are too tired to listen.

Man: Well, I come in from a hard day's work and all I get is what the kids have done wrong or what a difficult time you've had at the shops, or the car wouldn't start or something, and I've had a hard day too.

Counsellor: As I understand it you both feel you're working very hard now. Before your second daughter came along, and before Jim got his promotion, you both had more free time and more energy. That meant that if one of you had a problem the other was likely to have the time and the reserve of energy to help deal with it. That doesn't happen now – you've both got less time; you feel more tired and there are more pressures on you. That means in turn that something that might not have seemed so big in the past can now appear really annoying or really worrying, and if the other one doesn't *immediately* come to the rescue the problem itself seems magnified still further and resentment builds up.

Woman: Yes, I suppose that's what's happening, but what can we do about it?

Counsellor: Well, one thing may be to set aside some of the time you do have together to discuss things, and to decide in advance whose turn it is to give some of the problems an airing. That may help you steer away from both feeling you need to offload everything onto the other the very first moment you get together again in the evening.

Marriage guidance counselling will also have a part to play when a decision has been taken by the couple concerned that they must end their marriage. Then the role of the counsellor is concerned with mitigating the damage of divorce to the couple themselves and in relation to the future parenting of children.

Bereavement counselling

Bereavement counselling relates to the processes of grieving following the loss of a loved one. It recognises the fact that grief itself is a natural reaction to loss. The need for counselling interventions in such circumstances is heightened today because relatively few bereaved people will have the support through local family or church networks that was available in the past. However, clergy as well as other helping professionals such as doctors, will still often be involved in counselling in these circumstances.

The natural reaction of grief to a loss has been recognised (eg Worden, 1991) as involving a series of four mourning processes, or tasks. First is the recognition that the loss has actually occurred. Next is to go through the pain of grief, recognising and experiencing the feelings associated with it. Next is an adjustment to the practical implications of the loss, recognising the roles that were played by the deceased for the survivor and coping with their discontinuity. This might include learning new practical skills such as household budgeting or cooking. Finally, there is a phase of relocating the relationship with the dead person, which involves withdrawing some of the emotional energy of attachment, in order to move on with one's own life, and possibly to form new attachments.

Different people will take different times to accomplish these tasks and part of the counsellor's role is to appreciate the present stage of the bereaved person, so as to help them work through that stage and on to the next. Completion of one task appears to be necessary before the next can be commenced. Interactions between the counsellor and the bereaved person will necessarily vary over the course of these different stages. For example, in accomplishing the task of recognition of the loss, the counsellor may properly help by asking questions about the circumstances of the loss or by an accepting attitude when the bereaved person indicates a readiness themselves to talk about them. At the third stage of handling practical implications, the interactions will involve examining problems faced by the counsellee and how they might be resolved.

SUMMARY

1. Counselling interviews, most commonly one-to-one, are used in crisis situations and in other circumstances where a person needs to be enabled to determine their future course of action.

2. Counselling is usually seen as involving a series of steps, with the counsellor facilitating progress over an extended period often of months or years.

3. In non-directive counselling, pioneered by Carl Rogers, emphasis is placed upon maximising the opportunity for the person being counselled to form their own views about their situation.

4. Redundancy counselling may be conducted by people within the employing organisation or by external consultants. Use may be made of various facilities in addition to the counselling interview as such, including psychometric instruments and secretarial support for job hunting.

5. Vocational guidance counselling involves helping people understand what jobs or careers best suit their interests, aspirations and abilities. Paper and pencil instruments are often used to support these deliberations.

6. Counselling provision in the workplace may be general, reflecting an awareness of the need to help people deal with stress. There is also the provision of post-traumatic counselling focused specifically on those who have experienced disasters or major crime in the course of their work.

7. Marriage guidance may help prevent the breakup of a marriage or may ease the transition through divorce if the breakup does occur.

8. Bereavement counselling begins by recognising grief as a natural concomitant of loss and focuses on counselling the bereaved through the successive natural tasks of mourning.

7
Shifting the focus

INTRODUCTION

So far in this book the focus of most interviews described has been upon the individual: that is, the person being interviewed has been regarded as the subject of information about themselves. (The exception to this was in Chapter 3 where we considered interviewing undertaken in the design of structured interviews.) In the present chapter the emphasis is on those interview situations in which interviewees provide information which, by and large, is not used for decisions directly affecting them. There are, of course, some situations in which the two strands and purposes are mixed but some awareness of the possible separation of these aspects is important (see Figure 7.1). In all of the types of interviews considered here the key point is that the individual being interviewed is regarded as having some special information which can contribute to a body of knowledge and/or to decisions based upon that information. Such a person may not be unique in this regard and similar interviews may be conducted on a number of people.

JOB EVALUATION INTERVIEWING

A number of systems have been developed at different times for evaluating jobs – jobs are sized according to dimensions such as complexity, span of control and impact of decisions made. The outcome of such evaluations is used for a variety of purposes but most commonly for matters such as determining pay and grading. Armstrong (1995) captures this by giving a definition of job evaluation as 'assessing the relative worth of jobs as a basis for determining the internal relativities'. Necessarily, then, it is a procedure that tends to be applied in

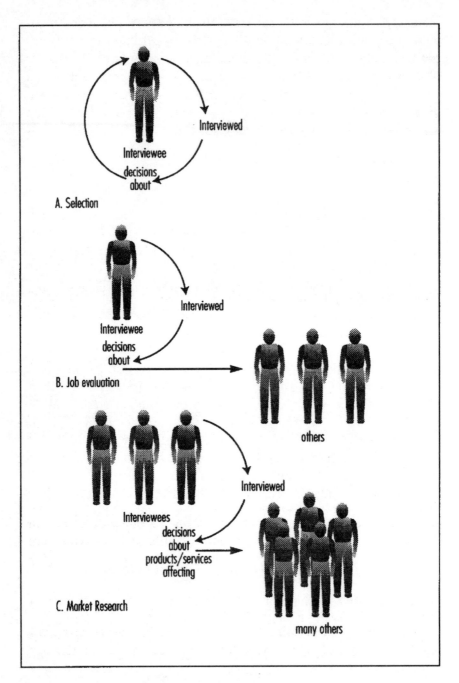

Figure 7.1 *Information flows and decision making in a range of interview applications*

relatively large organisations. Job evaluation interviewing and interviews conducted to determine the content of selection methods can both be subsumed under the heading of 'job analysis'. This is described by SHL (1995) as 'a systematic process for collecting and evaluating information about jobs'. Job analysis may include techniques other than interviews, such as getting job holders to keep diaries recording their work activities and then analysing their contents.

Grading and trading

Often in determining the eventual grade of a job in this way there will be a series of trade-offs and balances between different aspects. Thus a requirement for a very high level of specialist expertise may be balanced against the need to manage relatively large numbers of people, so that two jobs such as an individual research scientist and a supervisor of retail staff could, in theory, end up being evaluated at the same overall level.

In order to reach the evaluation interviews are typically conducted with those involved in managing the jobs to be graded as well as with those currently doing the jobs. Such interviews may be supported by reviewing existing documentation about the job. Thus where there are precedents for particular grade levels and well-established positions already in an organisation, the job evaluation interview may be little more than a formality leading to confirmation of an expected level. In other situations, for example where the job is new so there are no existing incumbents, there will be a requirement to explore the roles in more detail and in those circumstances the interview may well take the form of a structured approach similar to those described in Chapter 3, where required experiences, skills and behaviour are explored in depth. In addition to job content and responsibilities other matters examined may include patterns of hours of work.

There is, of course, the question of vested interests in evaluation processes. This might work in either direction. Managers might wish to boost their own prestige or remuneration by having relatively highly graded people reporting to them. Alternatively they might aim to contain departmental costs by keeping grades relatively low. Such considerations give reasons for having an independent job evaluation interviewer working within the confines of a pre-determined system. Such a person may come from an outside organisation or may be from a separate and specialised department in the same organisation as the job being evaluated. Working through the job evaluation process may involve elements of challenge, particularly with new jobs where there may be little or no previous experience to follow. Here the value of a standard system, objectively operated, is evident. Very often the approach adopted to finalise job evaluations is to appoint a job evaluation panel, some of whose members will be those who have conducted the necessary interviews. They will often be supported by an independent management consultant with special knowledge of the particular weighting system being used.

SELECTION DESIGN AGAIN

There are parallels between job evaluation interviewing and producing selection methods. In designing selection procedures, which will of course themselves often include interviews, the various competencies and situations that will need to be represented in a selection situation have to be understood. The methods commonly used, such as critical incident technique and repertory grid, have already been referred to (Chapter 3). Note that the application of such methods will, as with job evaluation, sometimes have a representational aspect to it. Thus there is a question of who should be interviewed about a particular job as part of this design procedure. Who this turns out to be may depend upon availability, and/or the need for their buy-in to the selection procedures ultimately to be used, as well as the information that they actually have to contribute. The choice of who should take part is rarely clearly laid down. This may be something that distinguishes the interviews required for designing selection systems from those involved in job evaluation just discussed. In the latter it may be very evident from the organisational structure just who should have a say, while in the selection situation this may often not be the case. Such decisions should most properly depend on things such as the impact of the role on various parts of the organisation, but this may not be particularly clear.

THE INTERVIEWEE AS EXPERT

In situations described so far in this chapter the interviewee is seen as having special knowledge to contribute and is put in the position of being something of an expert – the subject matter expert or SME, in critical incident terminology. In some interview situations this is taken even further, perhaps where a very limited number of people have the information required. Sometimes such experts are little aware of the particular expertise they have and so sophisticated methods such as the repertory grid may be used to explore this. Gathering information from experts is part of the development of so-called expert systems in which a computer program goes through diagnostic processes on a variety of information, producing reports involving conclusions or recommendations in a way in which the individual expert themselves might be supposed to have done. Such expert systems are quite widely applied in writing reports on candidates after psychometric testing. (For a discussion of this see Edenborough, 1994.)

Such approaches also have similarities to some procedures used in industrial design situations under the banner of Total Quality Management (TQM). For example in Taguchi techniques a variety of approximate methods are used rather than totally exhaustive design trials. Finding out what may be appropriate designs to experiment with may be achieved through interview methods with experts. Thus the interview may be seen as a way of leapfrogging what would otherwise be very lengthy procedures by using the expertise of the interviewee. In some of my own research during the early days of automation in air traffic control (Green and Edenborough, 1971) I used semi-structured interviews with air traffic controllers to capture their views on the current systems and explore design enhancements.

GATHERING EVIDENCE IN LEGAL PROCEEDINGS

An area in which interviewing has been established for a long time is that of legal process. When this involves questioning of a suspect or a defendant as opposed to a witness then, again, the purposes of finding out information and coming to a decision about the person concerned are intertwined. This adds to the complexity of the picture and is one reason why a variety of rules have built up in different societies to help ensure that information can be gathered in as objective a way as possible and so that individuals may not be led into or forced into giving a false confession.

I'll take the Fifth!

Of course, by the same token, there have been through the ages – and still are today – societies in which systems are deliberately set up so as to encourage people to incriminate themselves. Thus the range of systematisation is large, from the extreme protection of the individual being interviewed given in the Fifth Amendment to the Constitution of the United States so beloved of movie makers ('I will not answer that question on the grounds that I may incriminate myself'), to the show trials of Stalin's era in the former Soviet Union.

At the time of writing, in the UK there is considerable debate over the recent decision that a failure to answer questions in court may be seen as self-incriminating evidence.

The interview processes that are used at the end of the scale concerned with extracting confessions may be exceedingly coercive, involving threat and torture. Brainwashing methods have also been used to convince those being questioned that the suggestions put to them concerning their actions or those of their country in the case of prisoners of war, are in fact true. Such methods involve isolation, deprivation of sleep and very long periods of questioning and haranguing.

In the courts the total process of questioning by counsel on both sides may be seen as aiming and tending to elicit a fair balance of information (evidence). Along the way, though, the lawyers may by their questioning seek to discredit a witness or plaintiff. One task of the judge or magistrate in such proceedings is to maintain the balance by controlling the questioning and, if necessary, directing a jury to disregard answers to some questions. There are, in fact, strict rules governing how questions may be asked in court. Thus counsel questioning his or her client may ask 'What happened next...and then what happened?', but not 'Did you see him hit him?', which would be leading. Appeal procedures, of course, often make reference to inappropriate questioning either during police interviews or in court.

SURVEY INTERVIEWING

In surveys the focus is upon predicting the behaviour of a large group of people from the responses of a relatively small number. In order for representative responses to be gathered it is necessary to balance statistical samples appropriately; that is, the sample needs to be a microcosm – say in terms of gender, ethnic origin or age distribution – of the population of interest. Only in this way can one properly draw from the comments of the few conclusions about the behaviour of many.

Also, as in all other interviewing, the way in which questions are phrased and worded is significant in determining how successful one is in gathering relevant information. Eysenck (1953) relates the story of the polling agency who asked the following question; 'Do you think King George of Greece should be allowed to return to his country?' The majority of respondents replied in the affirmative. Another agency asked which of their respondents had ever heard of King George, and found that few had, suggesting limited value in the first question about the exiled monarch.

SURVEY INTERVIEW METHODS

A wide range of methods and techniques is used in surveys. Some concentrate on individuals and others involve working with groups. As well as variations in how questions are framed, there are also variations in how responses are collected. A number of these methods are now explored.

Focus groups

In a focus group a number of individuals are gathered together and their views on an issue are explored. Very often the comments made are recorded on tape and then transcribed for subsequent analysis. It is not uncommon for two facilitators to run the group, with one steering the discussion and the other making notes to supplement the recording. The discussion is led in accordance with some pre-set questions but issues that come up are explored further. Sometimes these may be matters not originally on the agenda but which may be of interest. I have experienced running a focus group with public sector employees, ostensibly on the subject of training. I found that the meeting would scarcely progress until those present had got off their chest a whole series of gripes about remuneration. This experience was repeated in the same project with virtually every group involved, with respondents seeing the external research team as representing management[1].

---

[1] I saw a television programme about Yorkshire Water and the difficulties they faced with supply during the hot summer of 1995. One interviewee, when asked for her views, persisted in linking the TV interviewer with the company in question, despite his attempts to explain that he was a wholly independent journalist!

With another public sector group who had, in fact, had a widely publicised and damaging pay dispute going for some time, a comparable series of focus groups raised not a single reference to pay!

One advantage of the focus group over one-to-one interview methods is that of efficiency in gathering several sets of views on one occasion. However, this is often less significant than the fact that different participants will have different views and the expression of these will stimulate further debate and discussion. This advantage also carries with it the potential disadvantage of one strong group member imposing views on the others. Albrecht *et al* (1993) discuss the need this implies for careful control by the facilitator. The subtle skills needed by focus group facilitators, or moderators as he calls them, are also discussed by Krueger (1988). He describes the control exerted as, ideally, 'mild, unobtrusive'. He also suggests the importance of a similar style of dress of moderator and participants to help establish rapport.

Panels

In panel interviews groups of regular users of a service are gathered together to discuss it in a relatively formalised way, sometimes using methods similar to focus groups. At one extreme such groups are self-governing and may, in fact, call in the supplier of services to hear their views. Thus they can scarcely be regarded as being interviewed at all. At the other extreme such groups will be taken through a particularly sophisticated questioning procedure. This may be especially so when choices are to be offered in relation to forthcoming services and enhancements. Panels may also undertake direct sampling of such services or products, for example tasting new dishes.

Face-to-face interviews

Face-to-face interview methods used in surveys may range from the 'straw poll' – in which a succession of available or loosely indicated individuals may be contacted for their views on an issue – to those situations in which a sampling structure is carefully prepared in advance and rigorously applied.

Face-to-face interviews conducted on behalf of an organisation and upon the general public pose some problems. Such interviews typically involve what are known as intercepts in high streets or other public places such as station concourses. Gaining co-operation at all and preserving confidentiality in such a public setting is difficult. It is also unlikely in such situations that any but the very crudest sampling parameters will be able to be followed. Thus one might obtain a balance of gender and a spread of ages, but the very nature of the particular setting used will impose sampling restrictions. Thus passengers at a railway station will be unlikely to represent a cross-section of motorists. They are also likely to terminate the interview when their train pulls in!

Telephone interviewing

In recent years the use of the telephone for conducting interviews has become increasingly common. It is particularly so for activities such as business-to-business satisfaction surveys, where a third party contacting clients on behalf of a supplier can be seen as being mutually beneficial. With such methods response rates may be very high indeed: figures in excess of 90 per cent are sometimes claimed. By contrast the use of telephone surveys in consumer work tends to have lower initial response rates. Again, though, the efficiency of the method and the scope to use appropriate databases, too, suggest that it may be superior to one-to-one intercepts. Thus with the telephone method the interviewer may start with a range of information about people and be able to access quite a large group at the outset.

With the business-to-business interviews it is sometimes possible to gain involvement of the interviewee for quite an extended period of time of up to half an hour or more. With consumer-related or political surveys a few minutes only is much more the norm.

A development in very recent years has been that of computer assisted telephone interviewing (CATI). In this the computer program steers and tracks the route through an interview, thereby permitting relatively complex branching among questions and enabling issues of some complexity to be explored more readily than by other methods. The interviewer sits at a console and keys in responses as the interview is proceeding. Results are thus very readily available for appropriate statistical analysis. Most organisations conducting sophisticated survey interviewing tend to use this technique. An example of part of a CATI sequence is shown in Figure 7.2. Interviewers who have experienced both methods commonly report finding the CATI approach by far the more convenient to use,

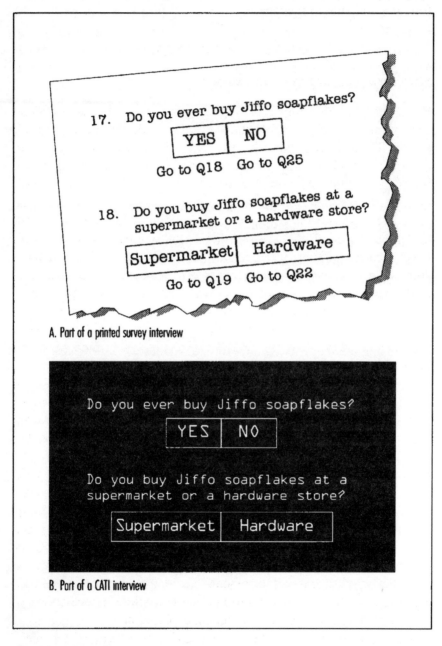

A. Part of a printed survey interview

B. Part of a CATI interview

Figure 7.2 *Market research interviewing without and with computer assistance*

obviating as it does the need to riffle through pages of questions to follow a branching sequence.

SURVEY APPLICATIONS

Structuring an organisation survey

For some years a number of large organisations have undertaken survey interviewing of their staff in order to determine a range of issues. These issues may relate to overall impressions (feel-good factor), or could be more particular in nature, such as looking at the impact of a company initiative in communications. Some organisations undertake these surveys relatively rarely and without a clear link back into management decision making. Thus they are seen as just one more source of information which can be utilised on a take it or leave it basis. In other cases they are closely integrated into management style even with reward mechanisms for managers being related to the comments received back. As such they have much in common with the 360 degree survey, in which reports from subordinates, peers and bosses are gathered to form a view of a person. (Although interview techniques can be used in 360 degree surveys, printed questionnaires are rather more usual.)

There are a variety of steps to be taken to prepare for the conduct of an interview survey in an organisation. Sometimes these steps themselves involve interviewing. Thus focus groups or the repertory grid type of interviews described in Chapter 3 may be used in early qualitative stages to explore dimensions of relevance to be included in a survey. These initial qualitative explorations will also be likely to look at relevant documentation, including organisational structures and statements, the results of previous survey interview programmes and any relevant literature on recent initiatives. For example, in companies that have recently undertaken total quality management (TQM) programmes, there may be interest in seeing how far messages such as those reflected in mission statements have been understood by staff. Examination of the content and form of these would be a necessary first step in framing questions for subsequent exploration.

As well as determining the playing space, as it were, of the interview survey, the initial work will also concentrate on some methodological issues. In some cases it will be appropriate to survey all employees, for example if a small workforce is being surveyed for the first time. In other cases sampling is likely to be necessary and it would be appropriate then to determine who is to be surveyed. This includes both the question of statistical sampling for representativeness and questions of inclusion, ie about which populations one is seeking to draw inferences. For example, if one particular group of employees has already been surveyed recently or their part of the company has just been reorganised, it may be decided not to include them. Distribution channels and briefing procedures to be used in advance of the survey will also need to be examined.

Following initial qualitative work the next stage is often a pilot survey in which interview questions are tried out. Questions that appear to lead to general difficulty in responding or where there are evident ambiguities will be discarded. The pilot stage can also be used to test the distribution methods used.

At the stage of the survey itself interviewers will need to be briefed in detail. This briefing will include giving them a script of responses to cover points of clarification that may be needed by interviewees. After analysis results are reported usually with a mixture of summary statistics and narrative comment. A sample survey structure is shown in Figure 7.3.

Scaling in climate and attitude surveys

As well as issues of framing the questions as such in survey interviews there is the matter of the response scale to be used. Experiments with a variety of scales were conducted in some of the early work in survey methods. Differences were identified, for instance, between those in which response levels given could be seen as cumulative – a technique developed by Guttman (1950) – and those in which people would rate agreement on bipolar scales with three, four or five points (Likert 1932). Different question types may be used with these very different response scales. When working in interview as opposed to questionnaire mode the number of alternatives that may be given are likely to be more limited. Examples of Likert and Guttman scaling are given in Figure 7.4 (page 116).

Political surveys

Political surveys may be undertaken in a variety of settings and for a variety of purposes. Perhaps most commonly known and the most

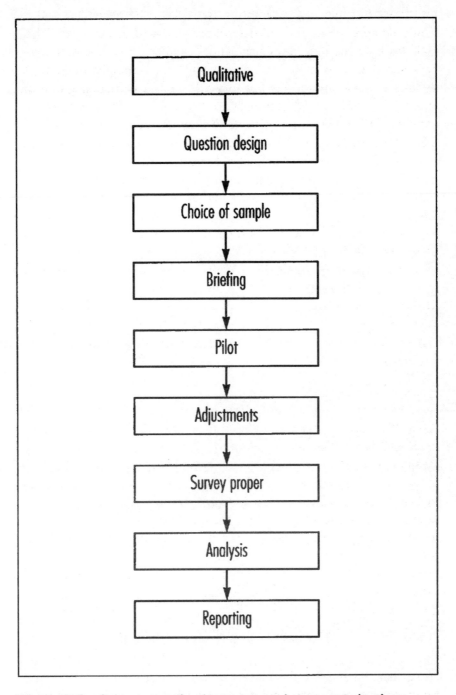

Figure 7.3 *Steps in conducting a survey in an organisation*

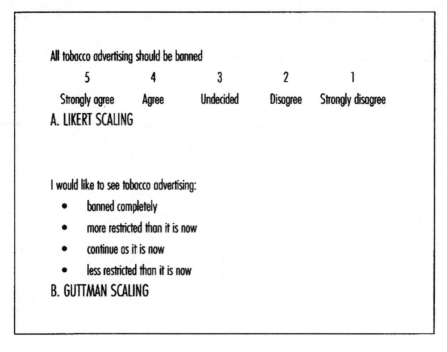

All tobacco advertising should be banned

5	4	3	2	1
Strongly agree	Agree	Undecided	Disagree	Strongly disagree

A. LIKERT SCALING

I would like to see tobacco advertising:

- banned completely
- more restricted than it is now
- continue as it is now
- less restricted than it is now

B. GUTTMAN SCALING

Figure 7.4 *Two common survey scaling formats*

widely reported are those that are undertaken to inform the public about the general standing of parties or individual politicians. Such surveys tend to become particularly focused on voting intentions around the lead up to elections and, despite frequent comments to the contrary, are keenly followed by politicians. In fact most political parties conduct their own surveys without publishing the results and will privately refer to these as well as noting those more widely available. Privately conducted political surveys may also be used by politicians in order to sound out the acceptability of certain political moves or the significance of certain issues.

Although the power of political surveying in terms of the effectiveness of its predictions was repeatedly demonstrated in the 1930s and 1940s in the work of people like George Gallup, there may still be difficulties in the accuracy of predicting results. Two main factors are, first, that the state of the parties either overall or in any particular constituency may genuinely be finely balanced. Hence differences found in voting may be smaller than the range of error inherent in any

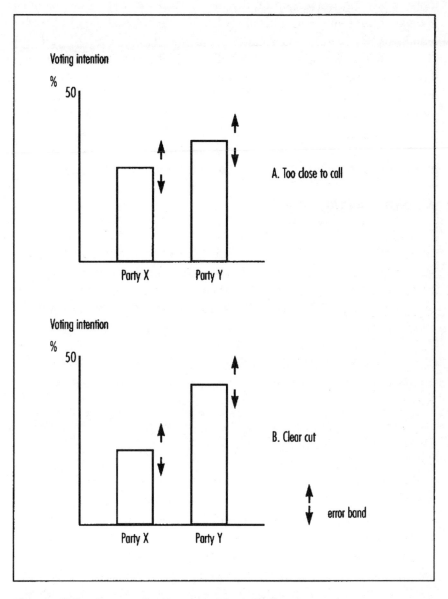

Figure 7.5 *Survey findings and band of error*

such measurement. (See Figure 7.5.) Secondly, in some situations the intentions of people are more volatile than others. This volatility is, of course, what is worked on during the feverish activity of an election campaign, so that greatest accuracy is likely to be obtained by surveys conducted as close as possible to the actual date or time of polling. The logistical difficulties inherent in this are, in some countries, confounded by limitations on the publication of survey results close to or, indeed, in the midst of voting. This will be particularly exacerbated in countries with a range of time zones. In such countries there are often restrictions on the publication of exit poll results, ie of surveys undertaken with those leaving the polling station, so that these are not allowed to affect the intentions of those voting later.

Political pseudo-surveys

In addition to individual 'straw polling' surveys, findings may also be derived from public meetings or studio audiences. When results of such surveys are published it is usually with caveats about their limited accuracy. Nevertheless they may still have an impact upon further opinion and indeed action. The idea of direct audience responses as a voting mechanism on TV, ie as a part of a democratic process, has also been suggested in the UK but not yet taken up in practice.

Customer satisfaction and market research interviewing

Customer satisfaction and market research interviewing have obvious links with one another. The difference is, perhaps, essentially whether one is looking at responses to what has gone before or what may be coming in the future. The distinction can be blurred in considering enhancements to a product or service and why these might be needed. In some customer satisfaction surveys the intercept method can be particularly powerful. This may be, for instance, in relation to a captive travelling public group or, say, people dining in a restaurant.

There are often quite complex methodological issues of interpretation. Thus in considering the surveying of patient satisfaction with experiences in a hospital the whole picture may be clouded by the degree of distress produced by an illness, the complexity of the issues that may need to be explained in relation to treatment regimes, or feelings of relief and gratitude for some degree of alleviation of suffering.

Customer satisfaction work may relate to a range of aspects or be focused on a single or a relatively narrow set of issues. Thus the organisation concerned may want to know generally how it stands with its clientele or it may wish to look at a particular area of service. It may also want to examine relative levels of satisfaction related to different service or product areas. Indeed some organisations publish internal league tables of such findings. In some cases research organisations will conduct composite satisfaction surveys covering several different service suppliers. Usually any one of these participating suppliers is given access to their own results and that of the group as a whole, so that they can compare their performance with their competition.

Market research uses face-to-face interviews, and focus groups and panels. As well as the intercept another face-to-face method used is the detailed pre-arranged interviews. These are targeted on consumers with particular characteristics, such as those who drive estate cars and change their vehicles less than every three years. Quite lengthy semi-structured interviews are used to explore motivations and triggers for this buying pattern. Once these are understood the car manufacturers can target their marketing on these points and maintain this part of the market as well as extending the targeting to others who might have similar motivations to be triggered.

Market research often uses sophisticated analytical techniques. Thus for products characterised themselves by a number of dimensions the questioning techniques may need to unravel these so that overall judgements may be broken down into different elements for action. For example, consider the interviewer helping to research a new chocolate bar, product X. She may ask an interviewee to compare it with existing products Y and Z, made by rival companies. Overall X may be preferred to Y, but Z preferred to X. It could be that Z has a reputation for quality that continues to keep it ahead of Y and X. If X is preferred to Y on grounds of price and both judged equivalent on quality, the manufacturer of X will face a dilemma. If he improves the quality (actual or perceived) of X he may still not match that of Z. At the same time he may lose share to Y, on grounds of price. In order to unravel such choices – and note that only two dimensions have been cited here – quite advanced statistical techniques are necessary.

One set of techniques was developed by Coombs (1964) for unfolding choices into their different elements. Other simpler methods are also sometimes used in market research, such as those based on

Osgood's Semantic Differential (1952). For example, using this a product would be rated by interviewees on a series of bipolar scales, such as hard–soft, good value–poor value, easy to use–difficult to use. Clearly with such techniques the interviewer has to follow laid-down procedures strictly, a characteristic, in fact, of most if not all of the interview processes discussed in this chapter.

SUMMARY

1. A distinction can be made between those interviews in which the interviewee is the subject of enquiry, as in selection, and those where the interviewee is a source of information.

2. In job evaluation interviewing, interviews are conducted to obtain information on a relatively objective basis, to determine pay and grading. In both job evaluation interviews and those conducted in order to design selection procedures the question arises as to the appropriate people to interview in terms of their representativeness, as well as their knowledge.

3. Interviews are sometimes conducted with those regarded as expert, in order to capture their expertise in a computer-based expert-system. Psychometric reports and medical diagnosis have been addressed in this way.

4. In legal proceedings interview processes are systematised but with methods varying to reflect different positions of defendants, suspects, witnesses and plaintiffs. The status of information – evidence – gathered in legal proceedings is often challenged, with continuing debate over what information given is and what is not admissible.

5. In surveys samples of people are interviewed in order to draw conclusions about larger groups. Question design and appropriate sampling are both critical to success.

6. Methods used in survey interviewing include focus groups, face-to-face intercept interviews and telephone interviewing. Focus groups are often used at the qualitative stage of survey design. Intercept interviews may pose sampling and other problems. Telephone methods include Computer Assisted Telephone Interview (CATI).

7. Climate and attitude survey design typically moves through a series of stages which will include qualitative and pilot work in advance of the survey proper.

8. Political surveys are largely but not exclusively focused on voting intentions. Despite well-established sampling and questioning methodologies, errors in prediction can occur when the true state of parties is close and/or when voting intentions are volatile.

9. A variety of panel and individual interview applications is used for decision making in product or service design. Statistical techniques used in analysis in this connection are often complex.

10. Customer satisfaction surveys may be used to check on the standards of delivery achieved and to plan service enhancements.

8

A variety of interview applications

INTRODUCTION

This chapter explores a range of professional uses of interviews. Very often in these interviews both the person *and* the subject matter are points of interest. For example, a politician may be interviewed to explore her intentions and to reveal aspects of her personality – can she keep cool in the face of adversity? Perhaps a linking characteristic of all the interviews discussed here is, though, that the interviewer operates from the basis of a body of knowledge and professional expertise. This is not a complete distinction, of course, from some of the other interviews discussed earlier in the book. Thus in recruitment the interviewer may be an industry specialist – particularly in an executive search – and some counsellors will concentrate exclusively on counselling. On the other hand journalists may be generalists or specialists in a subject. However, to a greater or lesser degree in the interviews considered here the interviewer brings some specialised knowledge to bear which is used in concert with their interviewing skills.

JOURNALISTIC INTERVIEWS

Interviewing the expert

As indicated in Chapter 1, interviews by journalists as a matter of routine certainly pre-date selection interviews. Sometimes there will be a strong focus on the individual being interviewed as a personality. In other cases, perhaps most particularly when a journalist is putting together a complex article, a number of people may be interviewed briefly but not all of them even identified by name. Sometimes when an expert is interviewed in this way their motivations for agreeing to undertake such an interview may be mixed. On the one hand there will be a desire to make a genuine contribution to the matter under discussion. On the other hand there may be questions of self-promotion, and something of this *quid pro quo* is often – but not always – recognised. It is by no means uncommon for people interviewed by journalists to see their words in print out of context or by implication associated with another individual. Sometimes retractions and apologies are printed but there is no guarantee that these will be read by those who have seen the original comments and so the damage is done! The only recommendation to those being invited to take part in such interviews is to go into them with open eyes and some agreement on what is to be quoted and what not.

Celebrity and political interviews

Whereas politicians may find it hard to avoid being interviewed if they are to maintain any shred of credibility, others of the famous – sports or entertainment stars or captains of industry – may find it easier to maintain their distance from detailed exchanges with journalists. The would-be interviewer may need to spend some time pursuing his quarry, judging when and where to phone or what subject to present as his reason for seeking the interview. A similar process of pursuit may be the necessary precursor to a first interview for an executive search company. While for the search firm with the right name their sign of interest may be a sufficient bait to entice many, much executive search work often involves painstaking enquiry and diligent pursuit. Sibbald (1992) entertainingly describes the hapless Schlock headhunter vainly pursuing his quarry, and managing to contact the wrong person at the wrong place and time.

Of course, the more celebrated the journalist the more willing the celebrity may be to be interviewed, so the work of tracking the celebrity down will be less difficult, and/or done by underlings. This does not mean that the celebrity interview is all plain sailing, even for the distinguished journalist. The famous often want to play things their way. I recall a piqued Muhammed Ali walking off the set of a live TV interview, and the interviewer announcing seconds later, 'he really has gone' with an air of disbelief. Very often the celebrity will have their range of pet anecdotes and if the journalist wants to avoid a repeat of last year's or last week's chat show on another channel they may have to work hard to get on to fresh topics.

If the celebrity interview is to yield material for a magazine or newspaper one approach is to acquire 'colour' in addition to the interview as such. Colour is provided by observing the celebrity's behaviour and his interaction with his surroundings, including other people. Thus if the interview were conducted over lunch in a restaurant, observations and subsequent comment might be made on what was eaten and what was said to a waiter or autograph hunter. With an interview conducted in the interviewee's home interactions with family members might lend the colour. Although far less formalised, there is an obvious similarity between the focus on behaviour here and that in an assessment centre (see Chapter 4).

In the interview conducted on radio or TV with a political personality, questions are sometimes seen as being angled or loaded, like the leading question in the selection interview, to present a particular viewpoint. However, when the journalist says, 'Don't you agree that the government must be in the wrong because it didn't warn people soon enough about the crisis?', the politician sidesteps. 'Let me answer that by recalling the actions of the previous administration', 'Let me answer a rather different point' and even, 'Crisis, what crisis?', are all ploys used, with differing degrees of success. The cat-and-mouse games that ensue often seem on the politician's part to involve avoiding admissions of fault, or definite commitment to future action. (Though not all politicians have learnt about the difficulties that can arise from pledging either 'new taxes' or 'no new taxes'.) Very often, of course, before such an interview takes place there has been some discussion of the approach to be taken and the likely avenues to be explored. To some extent then the process of challenge, evasion and pursuit which may enliven a broadcast interview may, cynically, be regarded as principally reflecting dramatic flair.

Another development in relation to interviewing a politician is the question of what may be stated on or off record. There is a practice, calumnified by some, of being able to hold briefings without attribution. Politicians or their aides are not quoted directly, so it is not clear who has been interviewed or given a statement. 'Sources close to', 'friends of' (more for royalty than politicians), 'unconfirmed reports' or the all-embracing, 'it is understood that' are all cloaks used. It is not clear what purpose this approach is meant to serve; it often adds to confusion and a number of journalists in recent years have refused to take briefings on such a basis.

An interminable diet of seagull

One interesting sidelight on this area of interviewing the famous is the format adopted by the BBC radio programme *Desert Island Discs*. In this a well-known person is interviewed about their life and a picture of their personality and interests is built up. The interview itself is interspersed with the interviewee's choice of music. The scenario is that the choice represents music that they would wish to have with them if shipwrecked on a desert island. They are also asked about what books, in addition to the Bible and Shakespeare, both thoughtfully provided by the BBC, they would like to have with them. The format can be seen as somewhat analogous to the projective techniques, described below under psychological interviews, where a stimulus other than a specific question would be used to provide a basis for further exploration. (I have expanded upon this programme a little knowing that today's broadcast media are highly fragmented and what would some years ago have been wholly familiar to all readers cannot now be assumed to be so. The longevity of this particular formula is, perhaps, best attested to by the fact that when the programme was originally introduced the shipwreck scenario was enlarged upon with the explanation, 'assuming, of course, that you also had a gramophone and an endless supply of needles'.)

Intrusiveness

Journalistic interviews have sometimes been criticised where they are seen as intrusive. There is a question of a balance here between what is really newsworthy and what is not, and even in respect of what is newsworthy how far one should intrude, for instance, upon private grief. McLaughlin (1986) writing on this subject agrees it is a tricky area but maintains the journalist's right to explore those issues that may be of genuine interest to a not merely curious or prurient public. He talks about explaining to parents whose children have suffered death or injury how their testimony might help save other youngsters. Of course it is not clear whether or not this is likely to be the case.

Exposing personal grief as opposed to presenting warnings in terms of facts may not go far to making the next child realise the dangers inherent in the stranger's sweets or the short cut across the tracks.

Intrusiveness is also, and more clearly properly, a characteristic of interviews conducted with those deserving of investigation because of their connection with some kind of deception or cover-up. Investigative journalists seeking to conduct this type of interview quite often face threats or actually experience physical injury or prosecution. The value of their work is well-attested by, first of all, the evasiveness of those whom they seek to interview and often by subsequent successful police enquiries and/or prosecutions. The interview, or interview attempt, is often the key to securing justice. Sometimes those who are operating outside or on the edge of the law are prepared in principle to give interviews but may have some wariness about who interviews them. This may apply for instance to those reformed (or unreformed) criminals who may be seeking to turn their notoriety into celebrity. It will also apply to protest or underground movements which have messages that they wish to see imparted to the world at large, but which are cautious with regard to their own security. In both cases the journalist may have to work over a period of months to gain the trust of those to be interviewed.

Promotional interviews

The promotional aspect of journalistic interviews has already been referred to in connection with the famous. In some cases this is taken further and an interview is, in fact, set up with promotion as a main objective. This is sometimes done successfully at events such as company conferences where an experienced media interviewer, who is very often a celebrity too, will interview a senior person in the company and help them get their views across to the workforce. The entertainment format of this may help deliver messages more effectively than a written report even in a chatty house journal or a more formal public address from the chief executive. Very often the interviewer will have some apparently challenging questions: 'How can you be sure that the upturn in business will be sustained?' or 'Does that mean job losses are likely?' but these will rarely be off the cuff. However, even if questions and answers are pre-scripted the format has the merit that matters of interest to staff and shareholders are clearly aired. Such interviews are sometimes captured on video for distribution within companies and may form the basis for further, localised, briefing sessions.

THE 'POST-EVENT' INTERVIEW

Interviews in event reporting

There is a class of interviews that are associated with a particular event or events happening. Many of these can be categorised as debriefing. At one end they shade into counselling situations, as when victims of traumatic experiences are encouraged to talk about and share their experiences as discussed in Chapter 6. At the other end they are much more clearly focused upon information, as when personnel are debriefed following a military mission.

The event may be a planned experience (for instance a training course), or an experiment as discussed under psychological interviews below. Alternatively it may be unplanned, as when the police interview witnesses to a road traffic accident. These interviews are usually necessarily conducted by specialists in the field concerned. Often they will work to a tightly prescribed format. For instance, in debriefing a test pilot following a proving flight in a new aircraft one would systematically explore views of the different systems and handling characteristics of the plane in the different manoeuvres undertaken. In some cases the format will be relatively open as when trainers, say at the end of a management development course, ask participants for comments. This has the advantage of allowing those present to voice any feelings of discomfort. The end of course review would frequently be followed, weeks or months later, by a further review in one-to-one format. This would still be in essence in debriefing mode, but now addressing progress in assembling or implementing development plans. Both the test pilot debriefing and the course review would often be supported by written questionnaires.

The exit interview

Another specific class of interviews within this general group, ie related to specific events, is the exit interview. Here an employee who has resigned is interviewed just before or even following their departure date about the reasons and background to their decision. Conducted internally such interviews are sometimes seen as perfunctory and as much a matter of form only as appraisal interviews sometimes are. It is commonly said, for instance, that people always claim to be moving for career development or enhanced pay prospects and never because they cannot stand the sight of their boss. There is, of course, a variety of sources of complication here. Any overt criticism of the boss could be seen as compromising a future job reference. Also someone who was not prepared to confront a difficult situation in the workplace may be even less inclined to do so once the need for doing so has been removed by displacement to another situation through the resignation.

Sometimes exit interviews are conducted by third parties and may even be reported upon in a cumulative way rather than individually. This approach may encourage the interviewees that their specific comments will not be attributed to them and altogether may provide insights with a statistical basis. When used in this way they can be regarded as coming within the field of survey interviewing discussed in the previous chapter. In this connection exit interviews may form a valuable part of the qualitative data gathering for a staff survey. If staff who have left voice particular concerns, be it over remuneration or sexual harassment, then inclusion of such topics in the survey may help identify groups of current staff potentially at risk of leaving as well as suggesting a need for remedial action. Such concerns might not be picked up in qualitative work with existing staff either because of reluctance to voice them while still in the pay of the employer or because, if not general, their impact would be diluted by the voicing of more common issues.

EXAMINATIONS AND INTERVIEWS

As referred to briefly in Chapter 1, historically all university examinations were undertaken in the form of a debate or interview between learned scholars and candidates: the *viva voce* examination. Such sessions might or might not be supported by written documentation. As time went on the written examination came more into prominence. However, the oral tradition was maintained, although sometimes in a somewhat haphazard way. Thus Ball, writing in the late nineteenth century (1880) about earlier practices, declared, 'Every candidate was liable to be taken aside to be *viva-voced* by any MA who wished to do so'.

The use of the *viva*, as it is commonly abbreviated, continues today in the university system. For higher degrees it is a major and for first degrees a relatively minor part of the examination method. Particular weight is placed upon the views of the external examiner brought in to see that appropriate standards are being maintained within the presenting institution. Particularly for higher degrees the examiners are likely to have been chosen because of their academic expertise and ability to understand the content of what may be a highly complex exposition rather than because of their skill in interviewing as such, and questioning techniques and interpretative methods are not tightly prescribed.

The candidate's thesis itself will form the basis for the interview but it will also typically range more widely across the subject area. For example if a particular scientific theory has not been written about, the examiners may explore whether this is as a result of ignorance or because it was not judged noteworthy. If the latter, the reason for making this judgement may be questioned and discussed. There is an indication of difficulty in utilising the information gathered in this way from a study in which the *vivas* for the International Baccalaureat were tape-recorded (McHenry, 1996). Judgements made from the tape-recordings were compared with those made directly by the examiners in the *viva-voce* situation. The former correlated more highly with other academic results, which could be attributed to attention being paid to irrelevant information in the face-to-face situation.

Interviews are part of other examination systems, such as foreign language examining, where the candidate's ability in the spoken language is assessed directly in this way. In the A-level system in England and Wales interviews are used to gain supplementary information in subjects involving project work, such as Theatre Studies. Such interviews seem comparable to the in-basket interviews used in connection with assessment centre methods described in Chapter 4. The academic tutorial system, in which questions are asked about a piece of work already undertaken, can also be seen as comparable.

INTERVIEWS IN THE HELPING PROFESSIONS

Sources of complexity

In a range of professions interviews are undertaken to find out information about individuals, as part of a supportive or helping relationship. These interviews come within general governing codes defining how the relationship should be managed and will themselves typically be subject to rules of conduct. The latter will vary in their degree of specificity according to the profession concerned. In all such interviews, whether conducted by a general practitioner, a lawyer, a financial consultant or other helping professional, there are likely to be several and broadly common strands of complexity.

To begin with the whole subject matter being explored may have a complex background to it. Thus the lawyer or the doctor may be seeking to extract information to make a diagnosis against a large number of hypotheses. The questions themselves may be straightforward – 'When did the rash appear?', 'Did you sign the agreement?' – but the overall set of possibilities and the data to be explored in connection with them could be vast. This complexity is itself likely to be increased by the fact that the person being interviewed will not typically have the same frame of reference, and so may be in a position to volunteer relatively little of relevance.

Another source of complexity derives from the fact that in these situations the person being interviewed, although they may have volunteered for the interview, may be in two minds as to how much they wish to reveal. Thus there are likely to be sensitivities around financial affairs, the background to, say, a dispute with a neighbour or partner, or the more embarrassing symptoms of an illness. The professional interviewer needs to work within the background of these difficulties and often with time constraints to extract the relevant information.

A further constraint in the GP's or other medical professional's interview is when the patient is not readily capable of responding. This may arise in the case of an accident or collapse where others present may need to be interviewed to find out what happened. It is also the case with a confused patient, a baby or young child. Veterinary surgeons, too, inevitably have to interview owners rather than the sufferers themselves. One of James Herriot's stories is of a group of children bringing their dog to his surgery and describing it as having been repeatedly sick. Only when they take cover as he handles the animal does he realise that what they are referring to is projectile vomiting; he is then able to make his diagnosis. (Further, potential complications have been pointed out by Coffey (1982), who describes how cats being examined at the vet's will purr to placate their threatening surroundings, rather than to show pleasure.) In all of these situations the third party may have a degree of emotional involvement in the situation that makes them a less than perfect respondent.

Interviews and the allocation of resources

There is a class of interviews where there is a requirement to assess needs and then allocate resources accordingly, often on behalf of a public body. This may be relatively straightforward, as when an unemployed person signs on for the first time for unemployment benefit. In other cases there may be endless complexities to unravel. For example, consider the local authority officer faced with a homeless family evicted from a council property in a neighbouring borough after repeated non-payment of rent, and allegations that they had been guilty of racial harassment of other tenants. In such cases the interviewing officer will be seeking to ascertain facts, explain regulations and possibly make a decision on resources, maintaining rapport and control throughout. The interview may start with incoherent negativity or abuse from the interviewee(s) and may need to be conducted in a tight timescale; *something* may have to be sorted out there and then, and there may be other applicants waiting. Mastery of the technical subject matter and a capability for firmness are only the starting points in these circumstances. Also required are efficient back-up information systems, well-established procedures and willing co-operation with a host of other departments and agencies. Thus, as with many of the other situations we have considered, the interview itself is only a part of the story.

PSYCHOLOGICAL AND OTHER SOCIAL SCIENCE INTERVIEWS

Projective and other testing methods

A brief reference was made earlier in this chapter to projective techniques. These are methods used by psychologists and others for a variety of purposes. The person being interviewed or studied is given some relatively ambiguous material upon which to reflect and comment. The idea is that the interviewees project themselves on to this ambiguous material, so that their responses reflect their attitudes, personality and typical behaviour. Best known of these approaches is the Rorschach ink-blot test in which ambiguous shapes are shown to interviewees who are then asked to indicate what they suggest to them. (The use of ambiguous material in question content was encountered in Chapter 4 in the discussion of the Structured Psychometric Interview.)

Projective methods have been used in selection and in counselling. In terms of the former, one application is the *defence mechanism test*, used for many years by the Royal Swedish Air Force in connection with the selection of pilots. This presents candidates with very brief exposures of pictures that can be interpreted as portraying threat. Those who recognise threat in the pictures are regarded as more likely to be aware of threats in the air and so more effective military pilots.

Interviews may also form part of some psychometric testing procedures. For instance, within the Wechsler Adult Intelligence Series some particular questions are asked orally. For psychometric testing of young children or people with learning disabilities an interview format is common. A mix of interviewing and paper-and-pencil psychometrics is also fairly standard in assessments by educational psychologists, for example in connection with dyslexia certification.

Interviews and research

In experimental psychology individuals (subjects) are asked to undertake a task and their performance is examined in the context of one or more hypotheses linked to a theory. For example an experimenter might have a theoretical view of how a stimulating environment helps learning. This could lead to a hypothesis that preferred background music improves learning while non-preferred music hinders learning. A number of subjects would undertake a learning task with preferred and a number with non-preferred background music and their retention for the learnt material compared.

Interviewing may be involved in this situation at the beginning of each experimental trial, to establish musical preferences. It could also be involved in collecting the data on performance if the experimenter were interested in learning expressed orally. An interview might also be held as part of a debriefing process after the experimental trial, to confirm the musical preference, to gain a rating of the difficulty of the task or to check that there were no extraneous influences. In fact very often these post-trial ratings are gathered by means of written questionnaires rather than interview. This may reflect experimenters' concerns that overly subjective impressions may intrude if subjects are asked to talk about their experiences. This concern stems from a host of difficulties perceived with so-called introspective methods which pre-dated experimental psychology as such.

In some studies on different cultural groups, for example those conducted by anthropologists, the interviewer is seeking to explore a society other than their own. This poses a variety of challenges. The researcher may need to work through an interpreter or alternatively learn the language of the group in which he is interested. Different societies will have different rules about who may be addressed at all, who can be talked to unchaperoned or what may be discussed with a stranger. Certain topics may be avoided entirely if questions are framed in the wrong way, or at the wrong time. It is said that Malinowski, studying the inhabitants of the Trobriand Islands in what is now Papua New Guinea, came to the view that they were unaware of the link between sexual intercourse and pregnancy. However, when he re-framed his questions and asked them in a different setting it became apparent that they were not so naive. Not surprisingly those undertaking such researches often spend very long periods – often several years – with the subject of their work and will complement their interviewing with observations.

Other formalised interview techniques

The repertory grid and critical incident methods discussed in Chapter 3 are among other interviewing tools used by experimental psychologists in their investigations. Another is the Q-sort technique. This method, first described by Stephenson (1953) involves a card-sorting task. Interviewees sort statements into piles according to how well they fit their view of themselves or someone else, depending on the application. Thus for individual personality assessments or psychiatric investigations (for example Block, 1978) it is how the interviewee describes himself in this way that is the focus of interest. In other cases Q-sort ratings are made about others by a number of expert raters acting as subjects. Then the ratings can be used in the same way as experimental outputs in testing hypotheses or in building up a theoretical position. The Q-sort was used in a longitudinal personality study by Block (1971) in which his raters assessed individuals in adolescence and in their 30s.

The sorting in the Q-sort is controlled so as to represent a normal or bell-shaped distribution (for a discussion of the normal distribution see Edenborough, 1994). Thus the 100 statements are required to be placed in nine categories, from most characteristic (positively salient) to least characteristic (negatively salient) as follows: 5, 8, 12, 16, 18, 16, 12, 8, 5. (This idea of a controlled distribution for ratings is one that we encountered in Chapter 5 in the discussion of appraisals.)

MANAGEMENT REVIEWS

Another area of application of interviewing is in reviews of management in connection with major changes. These include mergers and acquisitions, joint ventures or moves into new lines of business. In each case there is a group of managers actually or potentially in place whose capabilities and attitudes can critically affect the success of the changed or new operation. Looking at them individually, as a whole and in relation to other groups with whom they will have to interact can give the organisation leading the change a greater understanding of what it has just bought, what it might be buying or whether plans to launch a new product or service are viable with this team to implement it. Variations on this theme include assessing candidates for top jobs in an organisation newly acquired, say by a venture capitalist seeking to reorganise and redirect it. Ideally such assessments would be complemented by those on existing (or remaining!) management teams to understand the fit between the old and the new, the possible management challenges facing the new top person and how he or she is likely to manage then.

Limitations and risks associated with failure to undertake assessments in such circumstances have been attested to in a number of studies (eg Smart, 1998; KPMG, 1999). The need for such formal assessments was also something that I first raised in print some seven years ago (Edenborough, 1994). Their use, though, is still emergent rather than well-established. Among the difficulties often cited are those of access to the relevant people and problems of using what can be seen as intrusive methods. The former is certainly something of an issue in hostile takeover situations. However once a deal has been made this issue tends to disappear and does not generally arise in other change situations.

Intrusiveness may still remain a problem for some forms of assessment; for instance psychometrics could often well be contra-indicated. This points to the use of interview methods as representing an approach most likely to be effective and generally acceptable.

Structured interviews, as discussed in Chapter 3, are most commonly used in these cases. However their content tends to cover both areas of competency and some of the current motivations and concerns of those interviewed.

SUMMARY

1. In a range of professional interviews the interviewer uses particular knowledge to inform the approach taken and the interpretations made.

2. In journalists' interviews with experts, celebrities and politicians information may in effect be traded for a platform to make a point or to maintain a high profile.

3. Journalists' attempts at interviewing are not always welcome. The celebrity may wish to preserve some privacy, the dramatically bereaved to keep their grief private and the crooked to avoid disclosure.

4. Interviews following specific events are used to gather information about those events, sometimes to help plan future activities. Exit interviews may help shape policies and procedures.

5. Interviews have been used in connection with academic examinations for many years and, although less widespread than formerly, are still employed in this way.

6. Interviews conducted by members of a variety of helping professions are undertaken within a regulated framework. They are complicated by factors including unwillingness or inability of interviewees to co-operate fully.

7. Psychologists' and other social scientists' interviews may use specialised techniques or involve special materials. The focus may be upon the individual interviewee, as in assessment, or make use of a number of people in pursuing a research aim.

9

The future of interviews

INTERVIEW RESEARCH

Lots of studies, but limitations

As pointed out in Chapter 1, interviews are popular and, as indicated throughout, extremely widespread in their use. There has certainly been a lot of research into interviews but this has been limited in scope in relation to the very wide range of interview applications. By far the greatest number of studies have focused on employment interviewing, followed at a distance by those concerned with counselling and career development, appraisal systems and the like, and opinion formation as in market research. The field of professional interviewing – that of the lawyer or doctor – as a research area has been very largely neglected.

Even though studies in the employment interview can be numbered in hundreds, methodologies have been limited or flawed and the number of studies in itself may not be huge in relation to the extent of usage. As far back as 1954 Bellows and Estep calculated that some 150 million interviews took place every year in the United States of America. A few years previously, though, one of the first comprehensive reviews of employment interviewing (Wagner, 1949) reported that of 106 studies examined, quantitative evidence was given in relation to only 25 of them.

There is, too, the question of methodologies in research. There are difficulties of access of data and co-operation and, as Ulrich and Trumbo pointed out in their review over 30 years ago (1965), there are problems of separating out in research the contribution to predictions of success made by the interview as such, and other sources of data such as CV information. More recent surveys (eg Anderson, 1992) are still critical of research methodologies and models.

Such research that has been undertaken has more often than not attested to limitations in what has been called here the conventional interview. The contradiction between this state of affairs and the strong desire to interview was underlined by England and Patterson (1960) when they called for a moratorium on publications about how to interview until research evidence on the reliability and validity of interviews was stronger. The continued popularity of the interview is, though, everywhere manifest. Thus Bevan and Fryatt (1988) reported that of 320 UK-based organisations surveyed only two or 0.6 per cent never used interviews for selection and 82.2 per cent used them for all vacancies. A number of those reflecting on the continued popularity of the employment interview have speculated as to why it should be so persistent in use. In considering reasons, Arvey and Campion (1982) mention among other things the continued faith of interviewers despite contrary evidence. They go on to outline several studies in decision making which show how findings on interview limitations may be systematically ignored. This includes the relatively simple fact of employment interviewers actually receiving relatively little feedback about their judgement. They go on to make a plea for written guidelines on how to interview to be more evidently founded upon research results.

Most of those who have reviewed interview research in recent years have tended to point out areas that have been neglected. Thus Anderson (1992) claimed that the areas of impression management, dysfunctions in interview information processing and decision making and effects of different distributions of situational power were all under-researched.

Impression management – putting a good face on it

Impression management, or the conscious manipulation of the impact made by the interviewee upon the interviewer, has parallels in the field of psychometrics where impression management scales of various types, including faking good, are often used. As in that situation, though, the question arises as to whether impression management is necessarily a bad thing. Given that the interview seems calculated to reflect aspects of social functioning and these do have a relevant part to play in many roles, then some capability to manage impressions – you only have one chance to make a good first one – seems appropriate. It must inevitably confound science at the level of what research question should be asked, ie are we really interested in the impression made in the absence of such management?

One example of a study on impression management may serve to illustrate this point. Forsythe *et al* (1985) found that the selection of female applicants for management positions was influenced by their style of dress. Those in a more masculine style had a better chance of selection. Was this interview behaviour, whether consciously calculated or not, something which would be sustainable in work situations and with the same effect of creating a positive impression there? In fact Anderson himself recognised this point in reviewing the area of dysfunctions by saying that dysfunctions in perception may in many roles be effective latent predictors of successful performance.

Who is in charge?

The point about situational power is that the vesting of power in the interviewer unbalances the interview situation. Thus the interviewer is licensed to ask information in ways that would not normally be reflected in the interviewee's own scope for questioning. It would, for instance, be seen as OK for the interviewer to ask interviewees about their present salary, but not vice versa. This is notwithstanding the fact that interviewees might have a genuine interest in finding out about the pay for a job to which they might ultimately aspire. Indeed Herriot (1987) suggested that there should be a deliberate manipulation of the power dynamic, so that the focus of the interview started with acquaintance formation on something of an equal footing between the interviewing and interviewed parties. Changes in, and manipulation of, such dynamic aspects of the interview are, however, relatively unresearched.

The interview and the employment decision

Also unresearched and perhaps scarcely considered are the dynamics of the employing organisation in terms of the role of different parties to the interview and, indeed, the whole selection process. As a management consultant I have had many discussions with junior personnel officers (and indeed not so junior personnel directors) to the effect that management won't play by the rules. Planned interview structures are set to one side, arbitrary criteria are introduced and decisions made after the interview, sometimes even by people who were not originally intended to be involved in the process! This area, part of the sociology of the interview situation as a whole, seems to have received little or no research attention as such. It can be seen, perhaps, as linked to the question of ethics in interviewing. Fletcher (1992) pointed out that although much discussed, what does or does not constitute ethical behaviour in job interviews is not, in fact, well established. His survey of interview practice in connection with the university milk-round showed, for instance, 20 per cent of candidates admitting that they were seldom completely honest in interviews and 15 per cent of interviewers indicating that they felt it to be ethically acceptable to tape-record an interview without the candidate knowing.

There is work to suggest some of the factors strictly extraneous to the interview that may have a significant part to play in employment decisions. For instance Newman and Kryzstofiak (1979) sent CVs of a black and a white applicant to a number of employing managers. When the managers thought they were taking part in a research study they were in general more favourable towards both candidates and to the same extent. When they thought they had received details of genuine applications they were less favourable overall, and appeared to base their decisions on the applicant's colour. How the processes that these findings reflect could show themselves in interaction with an interview programme is, in the absence of research, a matter of speculation. Arvey and Campion (1982) saw questions of accountability and associated situational factors as a hole in interview research. It does not appear to have been filled subsequently!

Clearly future research in this field is likely to be driven, as much as anything, by equal opportunities concerns. Thus one could have a situation in which a strict interview procedure has been followed but its results set aside, that is, another process intervenes which may be prejudicial. The will to undertake such research may be precipitated by an increase in litigation about discrimination in employment and a shift in its focus. Currently in the handful of cases that are brought in the UK the emphasis is as often as not upon specific techniques of selection but not upon the interplay of these with the more shadowy aspects of employment decision making. Examination of relatively long-term records may be required to establish systematic discrimination of this covert nature. A specific factor leading to research of this type may be some of the positive-action programmes designed to remove inequalities in the workplace, such as the UK Government's

Opportunity 2000 programme aimed at increasing the number of women in senior management positions.

Further research in structured interviews

Structured interview methodology certainly seems to be increasing in use. As pointed out in Chapter 3, though, without research and control its more advanced forms can rapidly degenerate into an unresearched and uncontrolled procedure, perhaps being no more than a properly conducted more conventional interview, ie one pursued in the absence of the horror story dimension.

Further research does, though, seem likely in this field for several reasons. First, the whole of the competencies movement appears to provide a groundswell for structured methods and a recognition that they require to be properly set up. The SPI technique is ideally predicated upon this research being conducted afresh for each new application and this is a growing area. At the time of writing, there are at least five management consultancies in the UK alone working fairly actively in this field. For such research to be made more widely available may require the development of user groups and the like. It will also be important for those conducting meta-analytical reviews to be quite clear about the types of interviews that are being discussed and the research basis of these. For instance the practice in training in the use of SPI and, indeed, other structured interviews, varies from intensive courses for those making interpretations to a situation in which second- and even third-hand briefing of interviewers is given!

CHANGING PATTERNS OF EMPLOYMENT

No jobs for life

Much has been written about the changing nature of employment in the UK and elsewhere, with writers such as Handy pointing out some years ago now (1989) that some of the old certainties in the employment scene have changed irreversibly. For many, the supposition that employment was, if not for life, at least for a very long time has gone. Yet even now many of those in employment in the UK have been working for the same company for many years, so the full impact of changing periods of employment may be still to come. The overall picture is in fact quite unclear, with some writers such as Coutts and

Rowthorn (1995) while pointing out the extreme diversity of forms of employment in the UK, claiming that the trend towards diversity may have slowed.

Employment and interviewing

The effect of changes in employment upon interviewing practice are several-fold. To begin with, one of the areas in which conventional selection interviews have appeared to have been quite effective is exploring motivation for work (Ulrich and Trumbo, 1965). However, the form of this motivation now appears to be changed. Quite a lot has been written (eg Holbeche, 1995) about shifts in the psychological contract between employer and employee. What is claimed is that there is a move from a contract implying security and continued promotion in return for loyalty, hard work and continuing contribution to performance. This is replaced by a new psychological contract, one in which an employer seeks to enhance the employee's employability in response for flexibility and preparedness to make a variety of side-ways moves and undertake retraining but without guaranteed promotion (see for example Prior, 1996).

Nevertheless, it may still be that from the interviewee's point of view there will be an overhang of previous long-term employment expectations. Those applicants who have been unemployed for some time or who fear unemployment in their present role may be inclined to seek to demonstrate their potential for long-term commitment even if, in fact, it is unlikely to still be called for by their potential new employer. The same set of factors may well produce extreme caution on the part of interviewees. They may seek to explore the opportunity potentially on offer in some depth, to see just what sort of fire they may be jumping into if they leave their present frying pan.

Career management

The change in employment patterns also carries with it some other implications. The recognition by an increasing number of organisations that they have responsibilities in the field of facilitating career management is one. By career management is meant a variety of processes including career planning from the individual's point of view, and succession planning and other aspects of resource planning from the organisation's position. The increasing and increasingly professional use of procedures such as the career planning interviews discussed in Chapter 5 will be one aspect of this in the future. So too, seems to be an increasing recognition of the role of counselling interviews in general in relation to employment. Counselling will be required for those, still probably large in number, who will need for the first time to face up to the possibilities of periods of unemployment or major switches in career direction. Counselling interventions may also be triggerd by organisations recognising the fact of continuing change and the need for a wide exploration of new employment realities, both positive and negative for their employees.

Another sense in which employment-related interviewing will be likely to change is in relation to people working for organisations on a short-term, contract, project, temporary or seasonal basis. The motivations of these people will ideally be different from those of permanent full-time staff, and this will need to be reflected in the interviews. It seems unlikely that they could reasonably be expected to buy into the ethos of an employing organisation in the lifetime sense, as may have been required before. However, they may be required to have a value system which not only supports their pattern of employment on an individual basis but also supports effective delivery in these circumstances. Thus commitments to overarching concepts such as Total Quality Management (TQM) may be among the things that will need to be looked for in the future in the employment interview for this whole set of employees.

The changing employment scene seems likely to carry with it, too, an increase in the area of briefing interviewees for the interview situation. There are, of course, a variety of publications and other forms of guidance for those changing jobs, such as Parkinson's (1994) book *Interviews Made Easy* or Fletcher's (1986) *How to Face Interviews*. At present we may be at a transition point. I have been involved personally in both counselling and employment interviewing in the last few years with many who have said that they have not had to consider themselves for interview for 10, 15 or even 20 years past. That such people present themselves relatively unprepared and in a state of some anxiety in relation to the whole situation in which they find themselves is not surprising. Such a situation also, of course, implies the need for the various forms of grooming, practice and support for the interviewee.

CHANGING PRACTICES

Regulated interviewing

In Chapter 8 we discussed those types of interviews which are strictly regulated, with financial services being one example. At the time of writing, though, there is a considerable disquiet in the pension side of the financial services industry over the large number of people who have been poorly advised by those who have taken them through such interviews. Clearly, altogether, the process is not working well even though, perhaps, the relevant facts have been gathered in a strictly regulated interview situation. Whether this is likely to result in a sea-change in interviewing practice here or simply an extension of the regulation to post-interview considerations or other aspects of the whole financial advisory scene is as yet unclear.

In selection the debate on the ethics of interviewing has, at the time of writing, advanced little since Fletcher's (1992) discussion. It is possible that equal opportunities-inspired litigation and an extension of legislation on ageism may crystallise further what questions can be asked and the context in which they are interpreted and decisions made. On present form, though, it would be mistaken to look for overnight changes in the regulatory framework for employment interviewing.

In the field of medicine in the UK there is a major upheaval in terms of roles and responsibilities. We may again expect to see changes in the type of interviewing practices that are required. If primary health care is designed more and more to treat the whole person then the procedures to find out about the whole person's requirements may need to change. These changes may extend to developing different interviewing skills among GPs and the distribution of interviewing skills more widely among other health-care professionals.

The political interview

In the field of political interviewing much has been criticised in terms of the interviewee's – the politician's – tendency to avoid giving straight answers to questions. A variety of factors leading to widespread disillusion in present political arrangements may see some changes in the type of response deemed as acceptable from politicians being interviewed. Just how this will affect how the interviewer conducts him or herself is unclear. Political disillusionment is by no means new and may be cyclical. (The 1960s calypso-style Limbo song intoned *'Went to the market and what did I see – limbo, limbo like me – politician telling lies to prove his integrity'*.) Whether there will be new politicians paralleling the concept of the new man, and prepared to tell it as it is must still be questionable.

Customer-focused interviews

Increased business competitiveness and the continuing scope to use customer responses to drive business programmes seems likely to result in ever-increased use of the customer interview. There may be an increased need for regulation and control here, for instance to curb the common practice of making a sales pitch under the guise of a market-research interview!

The increased significance of customer research as a whole and within it the part that interviews will have to play is also indicated by the enhanced technological scope to customise goods and services. Thus historically in manufacturing, economies of scale were often the drivers of what was produced, as summed up in Henry Ford's offer, 'Any colour you like as long as it's black'. Today with scope for fine-tuning production and inventories with the use of a variety of methods including Just-In-Time (JIT), there are opportunities for very close customising, so that quite fine-grain customer information can actually be used.

SURFING THE COMMUNICATION WAVES

In discussing the structured interview methods in Chapter 3 I referred to an ongoing resistance to the use of the telephone. Certainly the scope to meet people and interact with them sometimes seems an all-pervading force driving the continuation of something like the conventional interview in many fields. (That this does not absolutely have to be the case is well attested by Clarke's work on the selection of undergraduates, described in Chapter 2.) The telephone has advanced as a piece of technology. It is now perfectly feasible to conduct interviews by phone with a recording of the interviewer and use of the standard key pad for entering multiple choice responses. Similar methods have, of course, been available for years for TV audience research. Resistance there will still be to such methods, (writing in 2001, six years after first drafting this book, I have again come across cases of extreme reluctance to exploit this piece of nineteenth-century technology in interviewing) but inevitably Luddite sensitivities seem likely to dissipate in response to competitive pressures. These techniques are, surely, likely to become commonplace in consumer interviewing and as indicated in this chapter moved into the screening end of mass recruitment, and then ... who knows?

Very commonly the state and convenience of transportation and communication technologies is relevant in determining how an interview is to be conducted. I noted a marked increase in enthusiasm for the telephone interview from a client who realised that his star candidate was fifteen-hundred miles away and for whom he required a report within 24 hours. Consider the case of King Henry VIII, who contracted an alliance with his fourth wife, Anne of Cleeves, before having seen her, ie without having interviewed her, and on the basis of the portraiture, in this case apparently unduly flattering, of the court painter Holbein. That this monarch's matrimonial alliances were unfortunate in three out of his other five attempts may suggest that a face-to-face interview would not have done much to change the situation. The point is, though, that in seeking an alliance with a foreign princess the King, and other princes of his era, were often obliged to dispense with the interview as a tool, and court portrait painters were quite routinely employed in this connection.

In addition to the post and the telephone, other technologies for distant communication are increasingly available but still relatively little used in interviewing situations. The exception is, of course, in the broadcast media where interviews are very commonly undertaken with people in distant studios or outside broadcast locations. Business tele-conferencing procedures may be increasingly used within organisations but the technology is not generally available for selection interviews as such. There may well be continued resistance to this. Tele-working in general is not widely practised and though it seems likely to increase in the future it is not clear that this increase will be rapid. It may be that it will take a major change, perhaps an environmental or transport disaster or some repeat of the early 1970s international oil crisis, to precipitate the use of these technologies more widely.

There will, perhaps, still be a hankering for the social interaction possibilities as per the subjectivist-social perception view of interviewing discussed in Chapter 2. This social element may actually be afforded by very high-quality technology in the form of interactive TVs and tele-conferencing services. Elements of counselling are, of course, routinely conducted remotely by the Samaritans organisation and it may, eventually, be more generally recognised that a physical presence is not necessary for an interview to be held. On the other hand again, E M Forster's 1911 story *The Machine Stops* depicted a society in which communication was remote, using a form of technology equivalent to today's e-mail and Internet systems and with voice communications as well as the physical delivery of goods and services. However, this multi-media society was seen as essentially carrying with it the seeds of decay and the story ends with the machine breaking down and the consequent rediscovery of the value of direct interaction. (It is of note, perhaps, that at the time of writing there is debate about the future of Internet shopping, with shoppers being found to be happy enough to browse electronically but still largely wedded to making purchases in person.)

Interviewing and the Internet

So what of the Internet in relation to interviewing? The ever more pervasive effect of this major technological development elsewhere seems evident. References to Internet addiction have been made for at least the last six years (see, for example, Hamilton and Kolb, 1995), with estimates even then of two to three per cent of the United Kingdom's online community spending most of their waking time actively using this medium. Its practical impact on the world of interviewing does not, however, appear to be enormous.

The psychological testing community has been much exercised by the possibilities and the difficulties. Thus Fox (2000) suggests 'the advent of the Internet – like the atom bomb – preceded the expertise to deal with the problems it creates'. Test publishers have been at pains to exploit the opportunities whilst managing the problems. Amongst the latter are questions of control, authentication of the person taking the test and protection of the publisher's intellectual property rights (Bartram, 1999). All of these are of course virtually identical with those applying in the case of telephone interviewing with a structured interview. Indeed if one takes the case of the SPI – as discussed in Chapter 3 – the use of remote delivery brings this even closer to Internet testing. One could argue that with the scope for simultaneous remote voice and/or text presentation whether one regards a particular tool as a test or an interview is merely a matter of perspective. Thus Bartram (1997) described AT & T's work in the use of voice response technology in terms of, 'candidates "dial a test" and the questions are spoken to them. They respond using their telephone keypad'. This sounds very much akin to the procedures described earlier in this section, originally, written in 1995, but which are described as interviews!

Perhaps the point behind this is that there may well be – though it really has not yet arrived – a blurring between the interview and testing via various types of increasingly sophisticated media for delivery, not least the Internet. One can also envisage the use of textual inserts and animations to the Internet-delivered interviews. This would be, for instance, a way of presenting the 'situations' in the situational interviews described in Chapter 3. Again this would seem to parallel some of the Internet developments envisaged by Bartram (1999), including 'realistic in trays'.

As yet, as in other fields, it does not seem as if the Internet will wholly support face-to-face interviews (see, for example, Sheehy and Gallagher's (1995) discussion of the limitations of technology in virtual communications networks). We are still for the moment at least, and as I said in 1995 more likely to find pluralist approaches to interviews, with a continuing mix of the remote and the face-to-face, notwithstanding some increase in the former. Regardless of the medium of delivery the interview itself in all its many forms will clearly continue to function as a focus point for discourse between people.

Appendix I

NAME: ALISON SOMEBODY

Overview

Alison Somebody is focused on end results and directed in her approach. She has a strong tendency to work to produce definite outcomes. She will be straightforward in her dealings with others and will generally carry them along with her. Along the way, though, she may not do all necessary to build rapport for the longer term. She appears to be interested in change and will seek to use it effectively to help gain objectives. She may be uncomfortable in situations in which she is not able to be in the driving seat herself and is likely, in fact, to seek a substantial degree of independence in her work.

Personal drives and motivations

Ms Somebody likes to have distinct goals and objectives, in the sense of having particular things to aim for. When she has achieved her objectives she will feel a sense of success. It will be important for her to have the opportunity of experiencing successes on a short-term as well as a continuing basis. To this end she is likely to break activities down into a series of sub-projects, each with their own clear goals, and to work towards these. She will also, though, have her sights clearly set on the longer term and will have quite substantial ambitions. It will be important for her management to recognise that she is personally ambitious and would wish to know that there is continued scope for growth within the organisation. This may be afforded either by prospects of promotion or by her having the opportunity to feel that she will continue to be challenged and given scope for personal development along the way.

Goals and targets are also important for Ms Somebody because they provide her with the structure for her work. She will be diligent herself in directing and controlling her activities in an orderly way and will probably wish to impose her sense of structure on others. Thus, a little paradoxically, it is not clear that she would necessarily fit in with the systems, procedures or even structures determined by her organisation. It may be important for her to be helped to recognise the degree of balance that the company will be prepared to accept in this regard and where they would insist that their predetermined ways of doing things are to be followed.

Perhaps not surprisingly, Ms Somebody is quite positive about change. Although not wishing to involve herself in chaotic situations she will see orderly and systematic change, in which she has a driving and central part to play as being critical for her success and that of the organisation. She will respond flexibly, we believe, and would be likely to produce new ways of doing things as she seeks to harness the possibilities afforded by change. She gave very clear evidence of a range of situations in which changes which others had perceived as overly challenging and, indeed, potentially disastrous, afforded her with the opportunity for finding new growth potential personally and in terms of the part of the business that she was directing.

Interacting with people

Ms Somebody has an awareness that she can sometimes be rather overpowering with others. On the positive side of this she has some-times used her tendency to be lively and combative with her staff and colleagues in order to spur them on to greater endeavours and successes. Thus she likes challenge and, to some degree, expects others to respond to challenges as well as challenging her on occa-sions. She is less comfortable, in fact, in working with and through those staff who require support. She sees this herself as an area of some deficit in her approach and has sometimes taken some steps to alter her behaviour. This having been said, though, it seems likely that she will continue to be rather forceful and, by the same token, not typi-cally empathetic at times. Continuing to surround herself with effec-tive others who respond positively to challenge is likely to be a more appropriate tactic than expecting her to shift her natural behaviour through 180 degrees. Indeed the awareness that she already has of tendencies to be overly forceful, challenging and hard driving may be as far as she will go in this direction and at least do a little to mitigate the adverse impact that her naturally forceful behaviour will have on some people.

Although independent, success-minded and tending to define successes herself, Ms Somebody will also appreciate recognition from others. These others will need to be significant and she may, in fact, not react well if what she sees as minor accomplishments are recognised by those who she would not perceive as of particularly high status or very effective themselves. Thus to some degree she sees herself as operating in a masterclass environment in which praise for business success is hard won but where, too, due recognition is appropriately given. Although material rewards appear to have some importance for her, these really seem to stand as symbols for recognition and have not, in fact, featured strongly in the motivational picture that we have seen.

Handling information

Ms Somebody appears to be systematic and also rapid in her approach to handling information. In gathering information from others she would tend to ask them about significant points or heads of issues. Then she will function in one of two ways, depending on the circumstances. To begin with she will be likely to form an overview, dismissing from further consideration those aspects of the situation that are not critical but seeing links between the main flows and direction of issues. For example she was clear about the balance between handling short-term change while still maintaining the company's core business strengths which, in fact, appear to lie in a relatively stable area of business. Having made her general overview of an issue or set of issues she is then likely to delve down into considerable depth to follow through further on specific topics. She is, perhaps, more comfortable in handling complexity when it is expressed verbally than in terms of numbers. However, she does not appear to be without facility in the latter area, although she would tend, where possible, to get others to do the donkey work in this regard.

Part of her orientation to change appears to be to build pictures of possible future scenarios. When she is doing this she will be likely to consider a very wide range of options and, in working with a team of others, will want to go through processes of brainstorming and speculation about ideas. She sees this work as particularly important for handling a changing environment. She sees her mental preparation at this time as putting her in a good position to cope with a variety of eventualities that come up and, indeed, appears to have done this quite effectively on a number of occasions in the past.

Appendix II
Some UK counselling organisations

Relationship counselling

RELATE
Herbert Gray College
Little Church Street
Rugby
CV21 3AP
Telephone: 01788 573241

Bereavement

Cruse Bereavement Care
Cruse House
126 Sheen Road
Richmond
Surrey
TW9 1UR
Telephone: 020 8940 4818

Other crises

The Samaritans
10 The Grove
Slough
SL1 1QP
Telephone: 0345 909090

General

British Association for Counselling (BAC)
1 Regents Place
Rugby
Warwickshire
CV21 2PJ
Telephone: 01788 578328

Note: BAC publish an extensive list of counselling organisations worldwide.

References

Albrecht, T L, Johnson, G M and Walther, J B (1993), 'Understanding communication processes in focus groups', in Morgan D L (ed) *Successful Focus Groups*, Sage, Newbury Park, CA.

Algera, J A and Greuter, M A M (1988), 'Job analysis for personnel selection', in Robertson, I and Smith, M (eds) *Advances in Selection and Assessment*, John Wiley, Chichester.

Anderson, N R (1992), 'Eight decades of employment interview research: a retrospective meta review and prospective commentary', *European Work and Organisational Psychologist*, Vol 2, No 1, pp 1–32.

Anderson, N (1997), 'The validity and adverse impact of selection interviews', *Selection and Development Review*, Vol 13, No 5, pp 13–16.

Anderson, N and Shackleton, V (1993), *Successful Selection Interviewing*, Blackwell, Oxford.

Argyle, M (1975), *Bodily Communication*, Methuen, London.

Armstrong, M (1995), *A Handbook of Personnel Management Practice*, Kogan Page, London.

Arvey, R D (1979), *Fairness in Selecting Employees*, Addison-Wesley, Reading, MA.

Arvey, R D and Campion, J E (1982), 'The employment interview: a summary and review of recent research', *Personnel Psychology*, Vol 35, pp 281–322.

Awosunle, S and Doyle, C (2001), 'Same-race bias in the selection interview', *Selection and Development Review*, Vol 17, No 3, pp 3–6.

Baker, E A (ed) (1949), *Cassell's New English Dictionary*, Reprint Society, London.

Ball, W W R (1880), *Origin and History of the Mathematics Tripos*, Cambridge University Press, Cambridge.

Bannister, D and Mair, J M (1968), *The Evaluation of Personal Constructs*, Academic Press, London and New York.

Bartram, D (1997), 'Distance assessment: psychological assessment through the Internet', *Selection and Development Review*, Vol 13, No 3, pp 15–19.

Bartram, D (1999), 'Testing and the Internet: current realities, issues and future possibilities', *Selection and Development Review*, Vol 15, No 6, pp 3–11.

Bellows, R M and Estep, M F (1954), *Employment Psychology: The interview*, Rinehart, New York.

Bevan, S and Fryatt, J (1988), *Employee Selection in the UK*, Institute of Manpower Studies, Brighton.

Block, J (1971), *Lives Through Time*, Bancroft, CA.

Block, J (1978), *The Q-Sort Method in Personality Assessment and Psychiatric Research*, Consulting Psychologists' Press, Palo Alto, CA.

Boyatzis, R (1982), *The Competent Manager*, Wiley, New York.

Boyle, S (1997), 'Researching the selection interview', *Selection and Development Review*, Vol 13, No 4, pp 15–17.

Brindle, L (1992), 'The redundant executive – typical or talented', *Selection and Development Review*, Vol 8, No 6, pp 2–4, The British Psychological Society, Leicester.

British Association for Counselling (1993), *Code of Ethics and Practice for Counsellors*, British Association for Counselling, Rugby.

Burnett, J (1977), 'What is counselling?' in A G Watts (ed) *Counselling at Work*, Bedford Square Press, London.

Campbell, D P (1974), *Manual For the Strong – Campbell Interest Inventory*, Stanford University Press, Stanford, CA.

Clarke, A D B (1996), *Personal communication.*

Clifton, D O, Hollingsworth, F L and Hall, E (1952), 'A projective technique to determine positive and negative attitudes towards people in a real-life situation', *Journal of Educational Psychology*, May, pp 273–83.

Coffey, D J (1982), *A Veterinary Surgeon's Guide for Cat Owners*, Windmill Press, Tadworth.

Collins (1981), *Pocket English Dictionary*, Wm. Collins and Son, Glasgow.

Coombs, C H (1964), *A Theory of Data*, Wiley, New York.

Coutts, K and Rowthorn, R (1995), *Employment Trends in The United Kingdom: Trends and prospects*, ESRC Working Paper Series, Cambridge.

De Groot, T and Motowidlo, S J (1999), 'Why visual and vocal cues can affect interviewers' judgements and predict job performance', *Journal of Applied Psychology*, Vol 84, No 6, pp 986–93.

Deutsch, F (1947), 'Analysis of postural behaviour', *Psychoanalytic Quarterly*, Vol 16, pp 195–213.

Dryden, W and Feltham, C (1992), *Brief Counselling*, Open University Press, Buckingham.

Edenborough, R A (1994), *Using Psychometrics*, Kogan Page, London.

Eder, R W and Ferris (eds) (1989), *The Employment Interview: Theory research and practice*, Sage, Newbury Park, CA.

England, G W and Patterson, D G (1960), 'Selection and placement: the past ten years', In H G Heneman, L L Brown, M K Chandler, R Kahn, H S Barnes and G P Schulz (eds) *Employment Relations Research*, Harper, New York.

Evarts, M (1987), 'The competency programme of the AMA', *Journal of Industrial and Commercial Training*, January/February.

Eysenck, H J (1953), *Uses and Abuses of Psychology*, Pelican, Harmondsworth.

Firth-Cozens, J and Handy, G E (1992), 'Occupational stress, clinical treatment and changes in job perceptions', *Journal of Occupational and Organisational Psychology*, Vol 65, Pt 2, pp 81–88.

Flanagan, J C (1947), *Army Air Force Aviation Psychology Program*, Research Report No 1, US Government Printing Office, Washington.

Flanagan, J C (1954), 'The Critical Incident technique', *Psychological Bulletin*, Vol 51, No 4, pp 327–58.

Fletcher, C (1986), *How to Face Interviews*, Thorsons, London.

Fletcher, C (1992), 'Ethics and the Job Interview', *Personnel Management*, March, pp 37–39.

Forsythe, S, Drake, M F and Cox, C E (1985), 'Influence of applicants' dress on interview selection decisions', *Journal of Applied Psychology*, Vol 70, pp 374–78.

Fox, G (1996), 'Nondestructive use of assessment in guidance and career development', Proceedings Division of Occupational Psychology Test User Conference, British Psychology Society, Leicester.

Fox, G (2000), 'Putting tests on the Internet – problems and pitfalls', *Selection and Development Review*, Vol 16, No 5.

Freud, S (1901), *The Psychopathology of Everyday Life*, Monatsschrift für Psychiatrie und Neurologie, July pp 1–32 and August pp 95–145. Modern edition Penguin Freud Library (1975), Penguin, London.

Frisby, C B (1971), 'The development of industrial psychology at the NIIP', *Occupational Psychology*, Vol 44, pp 35–50.

Gifford, R, Ng, C F and Wilkinson, M (1985), 'Non-verbal cues in the employment interview: links between applicant qualities and interviewer judgements', *Journal of Applied Psychology*, Vol 70, pp 729–36.

Gough, T (1989), *Couples in Counselling: A consumer's guide to marriage counselling*, Darton, Longman and Todd, London.

Green, R G and Edenborough, R A (1971), 'Incidence and effects at the man–computer interface of failure to optimise the display', in *Displays*, Conference Publication No 80, IEE, London.

Guttman, L (1950), 'The third component of scalable attitudes', *International Journal of Opinion and Attitude Research*, Vol 4, pp 285–87.

Hamilton, K and Kolb, C (1995), 'They log on but they can't log off', *Newsweek*, December, pp 60–61.

Handy, C (1989), *The Age of Unreason*, Arrow, London.

Harris, M H (1989), 'Reconsidering the employment interview: a review of recent literature and suggestions for future research', *Personnel Psychology*, Vol 42, pp 691–726.

Herriot, P (1987), 'The selection interview', in P B Warr (ed) *Psychology at Work*, Penguin, Harmondsworth.

Holbeche, L (1995), *Career Development in Flatter Structures, Report No 2: Organisational practices*, Roffey Park Management Institute, Horsham.

James, W T (1932), 'A study of the expression of bodily posture', *Journal of General Psychology*, Vol 7, pp 405–37.

Janz, T (1982), 'Initial comparisons of patterned behavioural description interviews versus unstructured interviews', *Journal of Applied Psychology*, Vol 67, No 5, pp 577–80.

Kelly, G A (1955), *'The Psychology of Personal Constructs'*, Vol 1, Norton, New York.

Kirton, M J (1976), *The Job Knowledge Index*, Heinemann, London.

KPMG (1999) *Unlocking Shareholder Value: The keys to success*, KPMG, London.

Krueger, R A (1988) *Focus Groups: A practical guide for applied research*, Sage, Newbury Park, CA.

Krug, S E (1981), *Interpreting 16 PF Profile Patterns*, Institute for Personality and Aptitude Testing, Champaign, Illinois.

Ladurie, E L R (1978), *Montaillou*, Penguin, Harmondsworth.

Latham, G P, Saari, L M, Pursell, E D and Campion, M A (1980), 'The situational interview', *Journal of Applied Psychology*, Vol 65, No 4, pp 422–27.

Leeds, D (1988), *Smart Questions for Successful Managers*, Piatkus, London.

Lewis, C (1992), *Employee Selection*, Stanley Thornes, Cheltenham.

Likert, R A (1932), 'A technique for the measurement of attitudes', *Archives of Psychology*, 140, p 55.

Maier, N (1958), *The Appraisal Interview*, Wiley, New York.

McDaniel, M, Whetzel, D L, Schmidt, F L and Maurer, S D (1994), 'The validity of employment interviews: a comprehensive review and meta-analysis', *Journal of Applied Psychology*, Vol 79, No 4, pp 599–616.

McGovern, T V and Tinsley, H E (1978), 'Interviewer evaluations of interviewee non-verbal behaviour', *Journal of Vocational Behaviour*, Vol 13, pp 163–71.

McGregor, D (1957), 'An uneasy look at performance appraisal', *Harvard Business Review*, May–June, pp 89–94.

McHenry, R (1996), *Personal communication*.

McLaughlin, P (1986), *How to Interview*, Self Counsel Press, North Vancouver.

Mehrabian, A (1972), *Non-verbal Communication*, Aldine-Atherton, Chicago, IL.

Miles, D W, Wilkins, W L, Lester, D W, and Hutchens, W H (1946), 'The efficiency of a high speed screening procedure in detecting the neuropsychiatrically unfit at a US Marine Corps recruit training depot', *Journal of Psychology*, Vol 21, pp 243–68.

Morgan, D L (1993), *Successful Focus Groups*, Sage, Newbury Park, CA.

Munro-Fraser, J (1954), *A Handbook of Employment Interviewing*, Macdonald and Evans, London.

Newman, J M and Kryzstofiak, F (1979), 'Self-reports versus unobtrusive measures: balancing method-variable and ethical concerns in employment discrimination research', *Journal of Applied Psychology*, Vol 64, pp 82–85.

NIIP (1952), The Seven-Point Plan, NIIP, Paper No 1.

Oldfield, F E (1953), *Fruitful Interviews*, Mason Reed, London.

Oliveira, T (2000), 'Implicit logic in unstructured interviewing', *Selection and Development Review*, Vol 16, No 2, pp 10–14.

Osgood, C E (1952), 'The nature and measurement of meaning', *Psychological Bulletin*, Vol 49, pp 197–237.

Otis, J L, Campbell J H and Prien (1962), 'Assessment of higher level personnel V11. The nature of assessment', *Personnel Psychology*, Vol 15, pp 441–46.

Parkinson, M (1994), *Interviews Made Easy*, Kogan Page, London.

Peterson, C and Seligman, M E P (1988), 'Explanatory style and illness', *Journal of Personality*, Vol 55, pp 237–65.

Prior, D H (1996), 'Career management – current perspectives on a new reality', in Heller, R (ed) *Towards the Millenium*, Sterling, New York.

Ramsay, S, Gallois, C and Callan, V J (1997) Social rules and attributions in the personnel selection interview, *Journal of Occupational and Organizational Psychology,* Vol 70, pp 189–203.

Raphael, W (1944), 'A technique for surveying employees' opinions and attitudes', *Occupational Psychology*, Vol 18, pp 165–73.

Robertson, I and Smith, M (1988), 'Personnel selection methods' in Robertson, I and Smith M (eds) *Advances in Selection and Assessment*, John Wiley, Chichester.

Rogers, C R (1942), *Counselling and Psychotherapy*, Houghton Mifflin, Boston.

Rogers, C R (1961), *On Becoming a Person*, Houghton Mifflin, Boston.

Rogers, C R (1965), *Client-Centred Therapy; Its current practice, implications and theory,* Constable, London.

Rorschach, H C (1942), *Psychodiagnostics: A diagnostic test based on perception*, Huber, Berne.

Schuh, A J (1978), 'Contrast effect in the interview', *Bulletin of Psychometric Society*, Vol 11, pp 195–96.

Sheehy, N and Gallagher, T (1995), 'Can virtual organizations be made real?', *The Psychologist*, Vol 9, No 4, pp 159–62.

SHL (1995), *Best Practice in the Use of Job Analysis Techniques*, Saville and Holdsworth Ltd, Thames Ditton.

Sibbald, J (1992), *The Career Makers*, HarperCollins, New York.

Smart, D (1983), *Selection Interviewing*, John Wiley and Sons, New York.

Smart, G H (1998) *The Art and Science of Human Capital Evaluation*, G H Smart & Co. Inc., Chicago, IL.

Stephenson, W (1953), *The Study of Behaviour: Q-Technique and its methodology*, University of Chicago Press, Chicago, IL.

Sworder, G (1977), 'Problems for the counsellor in his task', in A G Watts (ed) *Counselling at Work*, Bedford Square Press, London.

Taylor, P J and O'Driscoll, M P (1995), *Structured Employment Interviewing*, Gower Publishing Ltd, Aldershot.

Ulrich, L and Trumbo, D (1965), 'The selection interview since 1949', *Psychological Bulletin*, Vol 63, No 2, pp 100–116.

Vernon, P E and Parry, J B (1949), *Personnel Selection in the British Forces*, University of London Press, London.

Wagner, R (1949), 'The employment interview: a critical summary', *Personnel Psychology*, Vol 2, pp 17–46.

Wallbank, S (1992), *The Empty Bed: Bereavement and the loss of love*, Darton, Longman and Todd, London.

Walmsley, H (1994), *Counselling Techniques for Managers*, Kogan Page, London.

Warr, P B (1987), *Work, Unemployment and Mental Health*, Oxford University Press, Oxford.

Wernimont, P F and Campbell, J P (1968), 'Signs, samples and criteria', *Journal of Applied Psychology*, Vol 52, pp 372–76.

Wiesner, W H and Cronshaw (1988), 'A meta-analytic investigation of the impact of interview format and degree of structure on the validity of the employment interview', *Journal of Occupational Psychology*, Vol 61, Pt 4, pp 275–90.

Wood (1997a), 'The interview: just when you thought it was safe', *Selection and Development Review*, Vol 13, No 2, pp 15–17.

Wood (1997b), 'The interview: it's still not safe', *Selection and Development Review*, Vol 13, No 6, p 16.

Worden, J W (1991), *Grief Counselling and Grief Therapy*, Routledge, London.

Wrenn, C L (1949), *The English Language*, Methuen, London.

Wright, P M, Lichterfels, P A and Pursell, E D (1989), The structured interview: additional studies and meta-analysis, *Journal of Occupational Psychology*, Vol 64, pp 191–99.

Zamyatin, Y (1993), *We*, Penguin, New York (first published in 1924 by Dutton).

Index

References in italic indicate figures

add = address